SCHOOL CHOICE

A SPECIAL REPORT

# *School Choice*

WITH A FOREWORD BY

ERNEST L. BOYER

THE CARNEGIE FOUNDATION
FOR THE ADVANCEMENT OF TEACHING

5 IVY LANE, PRINCETON, NEW JERSEY 08540

*Library of Congress Cataloging-in-Publication Data*

School choice : a special report / with a foreword by Ernest L. Boyer.
    p.   cm.
  Includes bibliographical references and index.
  ISBN 0-931050-45-6
  1. School, Choice of—United States. I. Carnegie Foundation for the Advancement of Teaching.
LB1027.9.S35   1992                                       92-40895
371'.01—dc20                                                 CIP

Copies are available from
CALIFORNIA/PRINCETON FULFILLMENT SERVICES
1445 Lower Ferry Road
Ewing, New Jersey 08618

TOLL-FREE—U.S. Only (800) 777–4726   FAX (800) 999–1958

PHONE (609) 883–1759   FAX (609) 883–7413

# CONTENTS

# TABLES

# ACKNOWLEDGMENTS

I WOULD LIKE TO BEGIN by acknowledging the outstanding contributions of Lee Mitgang, senior fellow of The Carnegie Foundation for the Advancement of Teaching and a veteran prize-winning education writer, formerly with Associated Press. For more than a year, Lee traveled to states all across the country, conducted interviews, sifted through school reports, examined the evidence about school choice, and described the findings with clarity and precision. Beyond this essential field work and analysis, he continued with the project to the very end, helping to draft and critique the manuscripts.

Lee Mitgang brought tireless energy and deep dedication to this report. It simply could not have been completed without his vast experience.

To my colleague and friend Robert Hochstein goes special recognition for his professional contributions to this report and his unflagging personal commitment to the Foundation's work. His efforts are always crucial to our projects, but his presence here this time was especially vital. I cannot thank him enough.

The heart of this report came from the hundreds of parents, students, teachers, and state and local school administrators who gave so generously of their time as we visited states and districts to learn more about school choice. And I owe special thanks to the fifty-one chief state school officers and their staffs for their contributions and insights, without which a comprehensive look at school choice programs would have been impossible.

I want to express my deep appreciation to John Falco, Director of Alternative Programs in East Harlem's District 4, who opened so many doors and gave so unhesitatingly of his time over many weeks and many visits to his proud district. Of the dozens of individuals who shared their knowledge of local "choice" programs, the following deserve special mention: Bert Giroux, of the Cambridge Public Schools; Susan Schacht, of the Federal Reserve Bank of Boston; Charles Glenn and Kahris McLaughlin, of Boston University; Bill Grippo and Dennis Clancy, of the Franklin Township, New Jersey, School District; Barbara Strobert, of Montclair, New Jersey; Julio Almanza, of St. Paul, Minnesota; and Peggy Hunter, of the Minnesota Department of Education.

I thank six Montclair mothers who talked with us for hours about what choice had meant to them and their children. I am grateful to guidance counselor Bill Griffiths; school bus operator Bernard Hemmingsen and his sons; editor Carolyn Smith of *The Alden Advance;* and students Michelle, Chris, and Lara, of Alden, Minnesota, for being so very generous with their time. The people of Randall, Motley, and Staples, Minnesota, also deserve special thanks.

Prof. John F. Witte of the University of Wisconsin and Tom Fonfara of Governor Thompson's office in Wisconsin were always available to help keep us current on developments in Milwaukee. In Massachusetts, state senators Arthur Chase and William Bulger, and their respective staffs, provided us with important perspectives, data, and updates on that state's "choice" program, as did Kathy Kelley of the Massachusetts Federation of Teachers.

I am indebted to Amy Stuart Wells, of the University of California, Los Angeles, for helping us sort out some of the constitutional issues surrounding private-school choice, and to Prof. Julie Underwood, of the University of Wisconsin, who provided crucial background on the legal aspects of the Milwaukee choice plan.

My thanks, also, to Robert Terte, of the New York City Board of Education, and Roy Campbell, of Teachers College at Columbia University, for their wise counsel, and to Bette Weneck, of Teachers College, who helped us hunt through dusty boxes of archives on East Harlem and New York City test data. I thank New York City superintendents Anthony Alvarado and Anton Klein for sharing their insights into the politics of choice.

I gratefully acknowledge David Rockefeller, Jr., and The Rockefeller Brothers Fund for supporting this project. Also, David Haselkorn, president of Recruiting New Teachers, Inc., provided initial guidance in setting the direction of the report and offered thoughtful comments throughout.

Vito Perrone was especially helpful with advice on Cambridge and the Massachusetts state plan. Gene I. Maeroff's work over twenty years on urban education and on East Harlem's program gave us invaluable guideposts. Sally Reed helped keep us abreast of developments in Illinois, and Mary Ellen Bafumo provided essential details about innovative schools. Paul S. Boyer made a valuable contribution to this report, especially in helping us put the school choice debate in historical perspective.

As always, I appreciate the staff here at the Foundation for their commitment and teamwork in getting the job done. Mary Jean Whitelaw and Lois Harwood were responsible all along the way for collecting and analyzing the technical data that undergird this report. Hinda Greenberg, director of the Foundation's information center, provided, as ever, constant support for our research. Lynn Jenkins contributed greatly to research, writing, and editing, especially in the last weeks under deadline pressures. Jan Hempel joined in the final editing, prepared the manuscript for production, and oversaw the process through design and proofs to bound books.

Jeanine Natriello, working with Bob Hochstein, managed the release of the report, attending to publicity and the subsequent responses. Louise Underwood provided unfailing assistance in organizing the flow of people and paper, and was the calm at the eye of the storm when work on the report intensified. Patricia Klensch-Balmer assisted with the information center's research. Arlene Hobson-Gundrum also helped with the release of the report. And everyone's efforts throughout depended on the fast, accurate word processing of Dawn Ott and Laura Bell.

The Wirthlin Group administered the two telephone surveys: Survey of Parents with Children Attending Public Schools and Survey of Public Opinion.

Finally, a special thanks to my wife, Kay, for providing, as always, the inspiration and insight that sustained this project and helped move it forward to completion. Her selfless support means more to me than I can say.

ERNEST L. BOYER

President
The Carnegie Foundation
for the Advancement of Teaching

# FOREWORD

*by Ernest L. Boyer*

O F ALL THE RECENT Carnegie Foundation publications, perhaps
none has been more important than this report on school choice.
The urgency of the topic is apparent. In the current school reform debate, choice has moved to the top of the national agenda. Programs in Montclair, New Jersey; Cambridge, Massachusetts; and, most
especially, District 4 in New York City have been widely praised. Thirteen states have approved school choice arrangements, and proposals
are being considered in other statehouses from coast to coast. Most significant, perhaps, is that during the recent presidential debates, the virtues of choice were affirmed by all three candidates.

As the momentum for school choice continued to build, we at the
Foundation were impressed by the appeal of the supporting arguments.
It's obvious that the decade-long push for school renewal has been
largely disappointing and that fresh ideas should be considered. It's also
true that teachers should be empowered and that parents should become
more actively engaged in school decision making. And who would
deny that children should attend schools that match their individual tal-
ents? Clearly, extending educational options is an idea whose time has
come.

At the same time, we became increasingly concerned that many of
the claims for school choice have been based more on speculation than
experience. We observed, too, that little effort has been made to report,
in a systematic way, on the problems as well as the progress in the
"choice" programs now in place.

We were especially troubled that school choice, perhaps more than
any other reform strategy, has become so highly charged, so ideological. There's an intensity, even a zealousness, in the debate on school
choice that smothers thoughtful discourse. Political concerns seem

more and more to outweigh educational objectives. In such a climate, we wondered, is it possible to examine school choice on its own merits?

The time has come to step back and examine how school choice is working. What do we know about the impact of existing programs? What lessons can be learned from them?

The report card, we discovered, is mixed. While school choice does not appear to be a panacea, we did find impressive evidence, especially in districtwide programs, that it can stimulate school renewal. With proper planning and strong commitment, well-crafted "choice" programs can, indeed, empower teachers, engage parents, and improve the academic performance of students.

Statewide choice programs, however, have a less impressive record. Most of these initiatives have been imposed without addressing the school funding disparities across districts. Few states have adequately informed parents about the program or helped students who need transportation to their schools of choice. In this time of fiscal constraints, it is understandable why states find it difficult to address these crucial issues. Yet, unless they do, the promises of statewide choice cannot, we believe, be realized.

Private-school choice is not only the most hotly debated form of the program but also the most difficult to assess. Only one city—Milwaukee—has such a program. Information on its impact is sketchy, primarily because of the limited time the plan has been in place. Yet our review of available evidence and our conversations with those involved led us to conclude that, thus far, promises have outdistanced reality in Milwaukee. The lessons learned from this experiment surely must be carefully examined as the private-school choice debate persists.

How, then, should we proceed?

We're convinced the time has come for educators on both sides of the school choice debate to search for common ground. It's time to move beyond the ideological confrontations and develop a larger, more inclusive strategy for school reform—one that focuses not on school location but on learning, not just on choice but on children. Indeed, what strikes us is that while educators may disagree about the means of school reform, there is remarkable agreement about the ends. All believe that schools should be improved and that better learning must occur.

What we propose in this report is a strategy for school renewal on which all educators might agree. Let's acknowledge the importance of early education, empowered teachers, involved parents, an effective climate for learning, high academic standards, and continuous accountability. And let's consider the possibility of creating choices within schools, so that every school is a school worth choosing.

We must not allow the debate about choice to divert us from the urgent problems that profoundly affect the lives of children and diminish the effectiveness of schools. For while some of our schools are outstanding, ranking among the best in the world, others are desperately disadvantaged. These schools are failing not from bureaucratic gridlock, but from pathologies that surround them—neglected children, troubled families, and neighborhoods in decay.

Neither should we allow school choice to undermine America's local school tradition. From the very first, this nation has committed itself to community-based education, with citizens in each neighborhood coming together to support the education of children. This tradition has contributed profoundly to building our nation, and continues to sustain it. Today, even in our most troubled neighborhoods, the public school often is the only institution that provides a safe haven for children and an anchor point for families. Rather than talk of closing schools, we should look for ways to extend their influence, helping them to serve not just children but communities as well.

Finally, in the school choice debate, much attention is being given to helping individual families—and that's crucial. At the same time, American education has, throughout its history, focused not just on the empowerment of individuals but also on the building of community. No institution has been more central to that vision than the public school. Today our education system is far from perfect, yet dreams can be fulfilled only if they've been defined. And we believe the public schools remain the best hope for strengthening our democratic nation.

# CHAPTER 1

## *Freedom to Choose*

THE DECADE-LONG STRUGGLE to reform American education seems suddenly to hang on a single word: choice. Just a generation ago, freedom of choice was the rallying cry of those who clung to their self-proclaimed right to attend single-race schools. These days, school choice is a crusade with different meanings—and vastly wider appeal. Americans, it is argued, should be given a far greater voice in selecting the schools their children attend. Advocates of choice are promoting this option from the nation's most respected political and academic pulpits, driven by the conviction that public schools are in deep trouble and that bold, creative steps are needed to shake up a lethargic education system.

Choice has, without question, emerged as the single most rousing idea in the current school reform effort. In less than five years, thirteen states have established ''choice'' plans of one kind or another. Minnesota led the way in 1987. Michigan and Ohio passed laws on school choice that are scheduled to take effect in 1993. A dozen other states are debating the pros and cons of choice. Scores of individual districts, too, have introduced a variety of school choice arrangements. And shining above them all is Community School District 4 in the East Harlem section of New York City, which is routinely offered as proof that choice can benefit the nation's most downtrodden districts.

School choice comes in a variety of forms. First, there is the *districtwide* model, which permits parents and students to select a public school *within* their home district. Typically, specialty schools are established, and parents choose from among them. Local administrators, in turn, grant or deny such requests based on available space and, in some instances, on the need to achieve racial balance. This procedure is actually an expanded version of the magnet school idea, which was

1

sparked by the voluntary desegregation movement two decades or more ago. Cambridge, Boston, Lowell, and Lawrence, Massachusetts; Montclair, New Jersey; Eugene, Oregon; Seattle, Washington; Buffalo, Rochester, and White Plains, New York; Prince Georges County, Maryland; Minneapolis and St. Paul, Minnesota; and District 4 in New York City are among the notable examples of districtwide choice. In recent months, the superintendents of two of the nation's largest cities, New York and Washington, D.C., also have proposed to implement such plans.

Second, there is *statewide* choice. Under this program, students can attend public schools outside their home districts with the understanding that their selections may be restricted by available space, desegregation requirements, and by the students' ability to travel to preferred schools. Typically, districts that lose students also lose state funding. Until about five years ago, interdistrict ''choice'' plans were limited mainly to big cities and surrounding suburbs that were seeking to achieve racial integration. In recent years, however, thirteen legislatures, led by Minnesota, have adopted statewide plans and another twenty-one have considered them. The goal: to expand educational options for all students.

Third, there is *private-school* choice, by far the most hotly disputed form. This arrangement, often called a voucher plan, permits parents to send their children to private schools, using public funds. At present, only Milwaukee, Wisconsin, has implemented such a plan. In November 1992, Colorado voters rejected by a two-to-one margin a ballot measure that would have made their state the first in the nation to make this kind of program available statewide. The Colorado proposal would have given vouchers worth up to $2,500 to parents who send their children to private or parochial schools or who educate their children at home. At the federal level, President Bush, as a centerpiece of his school reform package, asked Congress for $230 million in fiscal year 1992 to support ''choice'' programs involving private schools. Another initiative from that administration, called the ''G.I. Bill for Children,'' would give $1,000 vouchers, usable at public or private schools, to as many as half a million low-income families.

Beyond these three options—districtwide, statewide, and private-school plans—choice also has become a catch-all term for a wide range of alternative programs for gifted students, dropouts, and those who aren't making it in traditional classrooms. Choice has even been used to describe programs that permit high school students early entry into college.[1] The word has, in effect, been stretched to include almost any innovation in which categories of students, particularly those with special needs, can enroll in nontraditional programs.

In this report we define school choice more precisely: We focus primarily on those precollegiate choice programs designed to serve *all* students within a state or district—rather than some special population—and to promote school improvement through a competitive education model, one in which parents are free to select the schools their children attend.

How does one explain the recent upsurge of interest in choice? What arguments are being used to justify such reform?

First, choice is being promoted as a key ingredient of school improvement. Giving to parents and students the right to select their own school would, proponents say, introduce much needed competition into a tired, monopolistic system. A recent Heritage Foundation report states it this way: "Transforming parents into education consumers will force the school(s) to shape up or lose customers. It forces teachers and school administrators to improve instruction and toughen standards if they are to retain students—and with them funding."[2] President Bush puts it even more bluntly: "For too long we've shielded schools from competition and allowed our schools a damaging monopoly of power."

Second, proponents insist that choice would give disadvantaged families educational opportunities now available only to the more affluent. "What better could we do for the poor, for those trapped in school systems that aren't working very well, than give them a little scholarship to vote with their feet, and send their kids to a good school?" asks former Delaware governor Pete Du Pont, who has campaigned relentlessly on behalf of choice.[3] Here's how U.S. Secretary of Education Lamar Alexander argues the point: "What we're simply trying to do is give people without money more of the same choices of schools that people with money already have, and that would include all schools—public schools, independent schools, private schools and religious schools."[4]

Finally, school choice is being presented as a fundamental right, one deeply rooted in the American experience. "In all aspects of our life we want choice," writes Ruth Randall, who, as Minnesota's commissioner of education during the 1980s, was instrumental in designing that state's trailblazing open-enrollment plan. "We can choose the religion we want to espouse. We can choose our grocery store and other shops depending on our needs and desires. . . . The one place in our lives where we have not been able to choose is education for our children from the time they start kindergarten through grade twelve unless we have money to pay for private school or for tuition to a different public school."[5]

Secretary Alexander has also embraced this "fundamental right" argument, insisting that the current practice of assigning children to schools is a repressive policy, contrary to our democratic way of life. "How we ever got the idea in this country of telling people where they had to go to school, I'm not sure I know. I think it's an aberration, an alien thought, really un-American. The whole process of choice in education would create competition, as it does in every other area of American life, and that would tend to improve all schools—not only for the rich, who already have choice, but for those without money as well."[6]

While advocates of choice agree on the virtues of the proposed reform, they differ considerably on its scope. Joe Nathan, an influential leader in the school choice movement and director of the Center for School Change at the University of Minnesota, views choice as just one piece of the reform puzzle, albeit a crucial one. Nathan, who helped shape Minnesota's statewide plan, argues that school choice need not result in jettisoning the existing public education structure. Indeed, he insists that choice programs should include such key ingredients as parent information, transportation for those who need it, and short-term financial support for troubled schools.[7]

However, other school reformers believe real change will come only if the existing governance structure is overturned. John E. Chubb and Terry M. Moe, co-authors of the landmark Brookings Institution study, *Politics, Markets, and America's Schools,* are the most prominent school choice theoreticians advocating this point of view. The fun-

4

damental problems of public education, they insist, are systemic. The current school governance arrangements are hopelessly crippled because they are under "direct democratic control." Layers of bureaucracy restrict the local school, and despite all the talk about restructuring, "the current wave of grab bag reforms leaves these institutions intact and in charge."[8] The proposed solution is a competitive market model, open equally to public, private, and parochial schools, and financed through tax-subsidized vouchers.

Advocates of choice also differ on the matter of accountability. There are those who support state or even national standards to assure that all schools offer their students a quality education. Others insist that externally imposed standards can, themselves, be obstacles to reform. Again, according to Chubb and Moe, statewide testing can be "a misleading and counterproductive means of evaluating the performance of schools." The marketplace should bring accountability to the system, and since parents are the ultimate consumers, the primary concern of schools should be to "please their clients."[9]

Finally, opinions differ on the potential of school choice. "Public school choice alone will not bring about all that is required to produce far greater excellence in education," says a recent report by the U.S. Department of Education.[10] Saul Yanofsky, superintendent of White Plains, New York, Public Schools, concludes that "choice is a means to a variety of ends; it is not the end." And Seymour Fliegel of The Manhattan Institute, a well-recognized advocate of choice, says that few would be so foolish as to view choice as a panacea for the nation's educational ills: "We have always maintained that choice is a catalyst, not a magic bullet."

On the other hand, Chubb and Moe are far more optimistic about the potential of school choice. "Without being too literal about it, we think reformers would do well to entertain the notion that choice is a panacea. . . . Choice is a self-contained reform strategy with its own rationale and justification. It has the capacity *all by itself* to bring about the kind of transformation that, for years, reformers have been seeking to engineer in a myriad of ways."[11]

Within the business community, too, varying opinions can be heard. David T. Kearns, former chairman of Xerox and currently Deputy U.S. Secretary of Education, declared: "It's important to remember that a functioning choice system, once it's in place, establishes new relationships and new attitudes. Parents no longer have to grin and bear it. . . . The message is clear—the American public wants a free market for education with choice and competition—they are ready for it. They believe it will work, and that it will strengthen the schools." Putting this conviction into action, J. Patrick Rooney, chairman of the Golden Rule Insurance Co., created a private voucher system in Indianapolis.

Others are more cautious. The Business Roundtable and the Committee for Economic Development, for example, believe that the problems of education cannot be resolved by choice alone. Also expressing caution is William Kolberg, president and chief executive officer of the National Alliance of Business, who states: "Market forces wouldn't operate the way Chubb and Moe suggest. Geography would impose a natural limit on choice. . . . Where would schools obtain funds for new construction, when today many are scrimping on routine maintenance? Would a school have any real incentive to expand, since neither principal nor teachers would be sharing any profits?"[12]

It comes as no surprise that school choice has not found enthusiastic support among many public school educators. Albert Shanker, president of the American Federation of Teachers, takes this position: "Choice views education as a consumer good—as something that I, as a parent, buy for my children from some vendor. . . . That goes against the tradition and values that have made our democracy the envy of the world. Education is a public good that communities have provided for all children because they are our future citizens." Reservations notwithstanding, Shanker has suggested that his organization would consider forms of public school choice. However, he rules out any plan involving private schools—a position also taken by the National Education Association.[13]

The National PTA cautions that choice must focus on the collective good of all students and warns: "If the dialogue about parental choice hinges on school improvement, this may indeed result in more effective education for our children. If the discussion is driven by the politics of the moment, we shall have again sacrificed improvement for a fad."[14] The National School Boards Association and American Association of

School Administrators have expressed their skepticism about choice's potential and staunchly oppose any plan that would send public funds to private schools.

Skeptics notwithstanding, school choice continues to be aggressively promoted by those who are convinced that school reform can only come about by "sweeping away the old institutions and replacing them with new ones"—"break-the-mold schools," as President Bush called them.[15]

But before existing institutions are "swept away," it seems appropriate to pause long enough to examine the underlying assumptions about school choice and discover just how theory relates to practice. Is it true, for example, that parents feel trapped in an "undemocratic system," eager to transfer their children to other schools? What evidence is there that school competition will revitalize public education? Does choice assure that the academic performance of students will be improved? And what harmful consequences, if any, are generated by school choice?

In response to these and other questions, The Carnegie Foundation launched a year-long study of school choice. In the course of our research, we contacted scores of parents, interviewed students, and talked with teachers and administrators in school districts and in states with comprehensive choice programs. We gathered information from chief state school officers in all fifty states and the District of Columbia, and visited districts with highly developed choice plans. We also surveyed more than a thousand parents to find out how they feel about the public schools their children now attend and to solicit their views about the desirability of choice.

In the next chapter, we summarize our findings. In subsequent chapters, we describe in more detail the districtwide, statewide, and private-school choice programs now in place. We conclude by proposing a more integrative approach to school reform, and reflecting on how the current debate about school choice relates to the history and social significance of American public education.

# CHAPTER 2

# *School Choice: Possibilities and Problems*

AFTER EXAMINING SCHOOL CHOICE PROGRAMS all across the country, we were struck by the scarcity of information about just how effective they have been. In states and districts where choice has been adopted, little effort has been made to record the process carefully or to document results. Anecdotes have been used to justify new initiatives. Sweeping legislation has been passed with little planning, and we were left with the clear impression that critical policy decisions are being made based more on faith than on fact.

Still, by looking at a large number of examples and reviewing data from a variety of sources, we were able to fit important pieces of evidence together. On the basis of this examination, we reached several key conclusions regarding the problems and possibilities of school choice. These nine findings are summarized below.

> *First, Americans in general feel positive about the idea of school choice. The vast majority of parents, though, appear quite satisfied with their current public school arrangements, and very few have elected to participate in statewide choice programs now in place.*

School choice is rooted in the assumption that parents should be freed from the current practice of assigning children to neighborhood schools. A market-driven model would make it possible for them to shop around for a more appealing institution. Given the centrality of this argument, it seemed reasonable, as a first step, to ask parents how they feel about the quality of the public education their children are now receiving, and to discover whether they would, in fact, like more options from which to choose.

With this in mind, we surveyed more than one thousand public school parents to determine their level of satisfaction. Eighty-seven percent said they were "somewhat satisfied" or "very satisfied" with the education their children received in public schools last year. We also asked parents whether they felt that the quality of education at their children's school was improving or declining. Thirty percent said the school was "getting better," and 15 percent said it was "getting worse." Forty-eight percent said it was "staying about the same."

Some school critics discount such optimistic judgments, arguing that parents simply cannot assess accurately the quality of their children's schools. Perhaps. But parent opinion cannot, we believe, be so easily dismissed. After all, with choice, parents are expected to make wise, discriminating judgments about the quality of different schools, often drawing upon fragments of information, or none at all. It therefore seems unreasonable to suggest that parents are untrustworthy when it comes to evaluating the schools their children are now attending—the ones they know best.

We do not suggest that the performance of public schools is adequate. There is, we believe, much room for improvement. Rather, we only note that the level of parents' satisfaction with their children's schools appears to be, for whatever reasons, quite high. But there's a still larger issue. What would parents do if, in fact, a school choice program came along? Is the eagerness for choice as broad-based as advocates suggest? To clarify this matter further, we asked parents: "Is there some other school to which you would like to send your child?" In response, 70 percent of the parents in our survey said "no." Of the 28 percent who did express interest in changing schools, 19 percent said they would like to send their child to a private school and 9 percent said they would choose a public school (table 1).

The depth of parent interest in school choice can be explored in yet another way. What has been the response to programs now in place? Looking at districtwide programs such as those in Montclair, Cambridge, and East Harlem doesn't help very much since, in these places, all parents with children at particular grade levels are *required* to make a choice. But in statewide programs where participation is optional, we found that fewer than 2 percent of the parents in any state have exer-

10

## Table 1

### Parental Desire to Choose Another School

"Is there some other school to which you would like to send your child? This school could be public or private, inside or outside of your district, with your child's grade level."

| | |
|---|---|
| No | 70% |
| Yes, private school | 19 |
| Yes, public school | 9 |
| Don't know | 2 |

SOURCE: The Carnegie Foundation for the Advancement of Teaching, Survey of Parents with Children Attending Public Schools, 1992.

cised their right to switch. We recognize that these low participation rates may not reflect the full depth of interest, since most state programs are relatively young. Further, lack of space in a receiving district and existing desegregation plans can also restrict participation. Still, in Minnesota, where the "choice" plan offers the widest range of options and has been around the longest, only 1.8 percent of the students have elected to leave their neighborhood school (table 2).

Finally, we were eager to find out the extent to which Americans as a whole, not just parents, support the idea of school choice. For the past four years, the Gallup Organization has sought to clarify this issue by asking: "Do you favor or oppose allowing students and their parents to choose which public schools in this community the students attend, regardless of where they live?" The proposition, when stated this way, has generally been supported by a margin of two to one.[1] In a September 1992 poll by the Associated Press, most respondents—68 percent—said that parents should be able to choose which schools their children attend.[2] Clearly, the support for choice appears to be quite strong.

It's not unreasonable that most people would feel friendly toward the idea of giving more options to parents. After all, having choices is deeply rooted in the American experience. However, when it comes to policy implications, it occurred to us that something has been left out. In supporting choice, what trade-offs are involved? We therefore decided to include in our own national survey a question asking the respondents to state how, in their view, American public education would

Table 2

Student Participation Rates in Statewide Choice Programs with
Comprehensive Plans

| STATE | NUMBER OF STUDENTS | PERCENTAGE OF SCHOOL POPULATION |
|-------|--------------------|--------------------------------|
| Arkansas | 1,667 | .4% |
| Idaho | 2,580 | 1.2 |
| Iowa | 5,227 | 1.0 |
| Massachusetts | 1,100 | .1 |
| Minnesota | 13,000 | 1.8 |
| Nebraska | 3,300 | 1.2 |
| Utah | 5,000 | 1.1 |

SOURCE: Information compiled by The Carnegie Foundation for the Advancement of Teaching from the Survey of Chief State School Officers, 1992, and other sources.

best be improved: by giving every neighborhood school the resources needed to achieve excellence, or by letting schools compete for students, with the understanding that good schools would flourish while weak ones would improve or close. The results: More than 80 percent of the respondents favored the neighborhood school approach. Only 15 percent supported competition. The rest said they either didn't know, had no opinion, or refused to respond (table 3).

In summary, the vast majority of public school parents appear to be quite satisfied with the education their children are receiving. Most are not inclined to move their children to a different school. And in states where choice has been introduced, participation rates are very low. The general public, on the other hand, seems to find the idea of choice appealing. But when asked to choose between local schools and a market approach to education, Americans overwhelmingly support the neighborhood school arrangement. None of this speaks to the merits or demerits of choice. What it does suggest is that the push for school choice does not appear to be a groundswell from parents.

*Second, many parents who do decide to send their children to another school appear to do so for nonacademic reasons.*

School choice has been promoted as a way to bring excellence to education. At the heart of the argument is the expectation that parents

12

Table 3

Public Opinion on School Choice

"Please imagine two people having a discussion on how to improve the public schools in this country. Mr. Smith says: the best way to improve education is to focus directly on supporting neighborhood schools, giving every school the resources needed to achieve excellence. Mr. Jones says: the best way to improve education is to let schools compete with each other for students. Quality schools would be further strengthened and weak schools would improve or close.

"Who are you more likely to agree with, Mr. Smith who would support every neighborhood school or Mr. Jones who would let schools compete for students?"

| | |
|---|---|
| Agree with Mr. Smith | 82% |
| Agree with Mr. Jones | 15 |
| Don't know/No response | 3 |

SOURCE: The Carnegie Foundation for the Advancement of Teaching, Survey of Public Opinion, 1992.

will choose schools of higher *academic* quality, thus challenging the low-performing ones to do better. However, this is not the way it seems to be working out. The evidence suggests that when parents do select another school, academic concerns often are not central to the decision. The Arizona Department of Education, in assessing the impact of choice in that state, asked nearly ten thousand parents why they chose another school for their child. Only about one-third reported that the switch had been made primarily for academic reasons. The rest said they made the move because of the new school's proximity to home, work, or day care, or other personal considerations.[3]

In Iowa, only about one-third of parents surveyed cited educational benefits or academic quality as the primary motive for exercising choice.[4] The evidence is less clear in Minnesota. A state-sponsored analysis of application forms in 1990 found that just 16 percent of the parents cited academically related reasons for participating in open enrollment; others cited factors related to geographic proximity, school environment, convenience, and other matters.[5] A more recent survey sponsored by the U.S. Department of Education found a far greater proportion of parents—55 percent—citing "learning climate" as a reason for switching. Many Minnesota school administrators disagree, however, asserting that geography and convenience are, in fact, the overriding motive for most transfers.[6] In Milwaukee, Wisconsin, par-

13

ents said they picked a nonpublic school for a variety of reasons, including educational quality as well as a greater feeling of safety or a desire for smaller classes. Further, our own survey of parents revealed that among those who do wish to send their children to other schools, only 15 percent identified "academic quality" as the reason. However, 11 percent cited "smaller classes" and 3 percent cited "good teachers" as the reason.

No parent would knowingly send his or her child to a school that is academically deficient. Educational concerns will, we expect, always play a part when decisions about choice are being made. The evidence suggests, however, that many of those selecting another school have other important considerations on their minds. One can rejoice that parents who wish to enroll their children in a different school—regardless of the reason—have the flexibility to do so. However, from what we've seen, it is difficult to conclude that choice itself will drive academic improvement through competition.

*Third, not all families have multiple school options available to them, and even when options are available the choice process tends to work much better for those who are most advantaged economically and educationally.*

The school choice argument is undergirded by yet another key assumption: that every family has within reach two or more schools from which to choose, and that at least one of these schools will offer a quality education suited to their child's needs. As an analogy, the comment is often heard that selecting a school is much like choosing a grocery store, or even a barbershop. Many options are close by, so the argument goes, and it's simply a matter of finding the one that's just right for you.

When it comes to choosing schools, however, the reality is quite different. Families living in densely populated cities may, in fact, have several options within easy reach, but what about those living in the suburbs or in rural areas? For them, the next nearest school may be miles away.

14

To clarify how geography affects choice, we asked parents to tell us how far it is to the school their child now attends. The median distance, we discovered, was about two miles. We then asked how far it is to the *next* closest public school. That median distance was four and one half miles. We also found that for one out of four families, the next closest school was far beyond easy reach, from ten to eighty miles away (table 4). And this says nothing about the *quality* of the next closest school. Given these conditions, distance alone rules out school choice for literally millions of children, unless transportation is provided.

In our own surveys, most parents said they could provide transportation to another school. Yet experiences in compact ''choice'' districts such as Montclair, Cambridge, and East Harlem show that this proves difficult over time. Publicly supported transportation will be required if ''choice'' programs are to succeed.

Further, we found that school choice seems to work best for better educated parents, who become better informed and are thus more likely to participate in the program. In Minnesota, for example, a recent study indicates that families using open enrollment are ''far more highly educated'' than the state population as a whole.[7] And a survey of those participating in the Milwaukee program revealed that ''choice'' parents who sent their children to a private school were more highly educated than nonparticipating parents. Specifically, 52 percent of the mothers and female guardians exercising choice had at least some college. For nonparticipants, only 40 percent had attended college. For fathers the difference in education levels was not evident (table 5). Overall, however, the results suggest that choice is of greatest benefit to the educationally advantaged.

The economic status of families also seems to be an important variable in determining how well-informed parents become about their options. In the affluent suburb of Montclair, New Jersey, where all parents of elementary students must participate in choice, we found that families with lower incomes (under $50,000) tended to use fewer sources of information to make their decisions than did higher income residents. For example, only about half of lower income families actually visited schools before making a decision. By contrast, 84 percent of the highest

Table 4

Distance to the Next Closest Public School

"Approximately how far is it to the next closest public school with your child's grade level?"

| | |
|---|---|
| Less than 2 miles | 25% |
| 2 - 4.99 miles | 26 |
| 5 - 9.99 miles | 24 |
| 10 miles or more | 25 |

SOURCE: The Carnegie Foundation for the Advancement of Teaching, Survey of Parents with Children Attending Public Schools, 1992.

income parents made such visits. Also, slightly more than one-third of lower income parents used written information about the schools; for the wealthiest families, it was 76 percent (table 6).

In short, school choice works better for some parents than for others. Those with the education, sophistication, and especially the right location may be able to participate in such programs. Others would be less well informed or be excluded altogether. For them, the choice pattern does not fit the cloth.

*Fourth, evidence about the effectiveness of private-school choice, limited as it is, suggests that such a policy does not improve student achievement or stimulate school renewal.*

Including private schools in choice programs is being vigorously debated. Those supporting the idea insist that such a program would benefit students educationally, bring added competition to the system, and make more options available to poor parents. Opponents argue that such a plan would simply siphon money from underfunded public schools and raise serious constitutional questions.

Setting aside these arguments for the moment, we wanted to know how popular private-school choice actually is. Recent surveys among *Americans as a whole* reveal growing support for the idea of using public funds to send children to private schools.[8] However, when we asked *parents of public school children* if they thought publicly funded vouchers should be used to enroll children in private schools, they opposed

## Table 5

### The Education Level of Private School "Choice" Parents and Public School Parents in Milwaukee
*(1989–90 and 1990–91)*

| | PERCENTAGE OF PARENTS WHO ATTAINED EACH EDUCATION LEVEL | | | | | |
| --- | --- | --- | --- | --- | --- | --- |
| | EIGHTH GRADE | SOME HIGH SCHOOL | G.E.D. | HIGH SCHOOL | SOME COLLEGE | COLLEGE OR HIGHER |
| **Private School "Choice" Parents** | | | | | | |
| Mother/Female Guardian | 3% | 12% | 11% | 22% | 45% | 7% |
| Father/Male Guardian | 9 | 16 | 8 | 28 | 30 | 9 |
| **Public School Parents** | | | | | | |
| Mother/Female Guardian | 8 | 18 | 7 | 28 | 29 | 11 |
| Father/Male Guardian | 9 | 16 | 8 | 26 | 27 | 15 |

*Note*: Combined data for two years.
Source: John F. Witte, "The Milwaukee Private-School Parental Choice Program," Department of Political Science, University of Wisconsin, Madison; paper given at the Economic Policy Symposium, Washington, D.C., 1 October 1992, table 3.

the idea by a margin of nearly two to one (table 7). In interpreting these findings, it is important to bear in mind that different questions were posed to different populations.

What do we know about the effectiveness of private-school choice? To date, only one such plan exists, in Milwaukee, Wisconsin, and thus far the evidence from that city is not encouraging. While most students and parents participating in the program say they are happy with their chosen schools, an astonishing 40 percent of students who made the switch to private schools did not return the next year. Further, the standardized test scores of participating students have shown little or no improvement in reading and math and remain well below average in

17

Table 6

Sources of Information Used by Montclair Parents
in Making School Choice Decisions
*(By Income Level, 1989–90)*

| SOURCE | PERCENTAGE OF PARENTS | | |
| --- | --- | --- | --- |
| | <$50,000 LOWER | $50–99,999 MIDDLE | ≥$100,000 UPPER |
| Talking to others | 90% | 90% | 90% |
| Visits to schools | 53 | 81 | 84 |
| Board of education materials | 57 | 72 | 84 |
| Parent evening program | 45 | 67 | 74 |
| Written information from magnet schools | 35 | 65 | 76 |
| Principals | 31 | 65 | 58 |
| Newspapers | 35 | 50 | 53 |
| Nursery school staff | 43 | 38 | 35 |
| Central office staff | 20 | 21 | 19 |
| Parent coordinator | 8 | 9 | 8 |

SOURCE: Barbara Strobert, "Factors Influencing Parental Choice in Selecting Magnet Schools in the Montclair, New Jersey, Public Schools," dissertation for Teachers College, Columbia University, 1990, p. 79.

both. We recognize, of course, that more time is needed to test the full impact of the program.

The Milwaukee experiment also demonstrates the hazards of introducing private-school choice without providing for public accountability. Proponents of choice argue that to impose state oversight on private schools would force them into the same mold that has restricted the creativity of public education. The argument seems appealing. Yet in the first years of Milwaukee's plan, one school shut down in a cloud of scandal, and the performance standards met by most of the remaining schools were marginal, at best. Participating schools are, in fact, asked to meet only *one* of four minimum standards regarding student attendance, grade promotion, parental involvement, or academic progress. Only one school reported on the academic achievement of its students.

Thus far, only about six hundred of the 97,000 Milwaukee public school students have switched to a private school. The program is limited to one thousand participants. Further, as a result of a legal opinion from the U.S. Department of Education, Milwaukee's participating pri-

Table 7

Parents' Opinions on Vouchers

"Some people think that parents should be given a voucher which they could use to enroll their child in a private school at public expense. Do you support or oppose this idea?"

| | |
|---|---|
| Support | 32% |
| Oppose | 62 |
| Don't know | 6 |

SOURCE: The Carnegie Foundation for the Advancement of Teaching, Survey of Parents with Children Attending Public Schools, 1992.

vate schools are under no obligation to accept disabled students. Simply put, while a handful of students may have benefitted, the Milwaukee plan appears, thus far, to have done little or nothing to help one of our most troubled school systems. Promises have outdistanced reality in Milwaukee.

*Fifth, parents and students who do participate in school choice in both the public and private sectors tend to feel good about their decisions and like the programs in which their children are enrolled.*

School choice, it is argued, will both energize schools and empower parents. We found that those who do select their own schools are, in fact, generally pleased with their decisions. The U.S. Department of Education survey cited earlier found that 95 percent of Minnesota's secondary school students who chose new schools were either "very satisfied" or "satisfied" with their selections. In rural Minnesota, parents told us they welcomed the opportunity to move their children from small schools to larger ones that offered richer programs of study. In East Harlem, students said the teachers in their schools of choice "really cared about them." They also liked working on themes of special interest, having smaller classes, and engaging in hands-on projects, all typical of the offerings in that district's specialized schools.

We met a troubled, angry boy named Jason who had been lost in a large, impersonal city school but found a caring friend in the principal of East Harlem's Bridge School. We remember 13-year-old Jennifer,

19

who said her safe, orderly alternative school "makes you feel respect-able." And a seventh-grade girl we met in Milwaukee spoke positively about the safer environment at her chosen private school.

Teachers also expressed their satisfaction. Indeed, the success of "choice" programs often seems to have as much or even more to do with teacher empowerment as with school selection. Science teacher Kathy Brown at the Peabody School in Cambridge, Massachusetts, told us that the plan in that district has made her feel "entrepreneurial" and helped inspire her to devise creative new programs for her children. All of this suggests that, whatever the motivations behind choice, the process tends to bring with it a sense of satisfaction shared by many parents, students, and teachers, too—an outcome that should surely be applauded.

A high level of satisfaction was found among parents participating in the Milwaukee program. In his annual reports on that program, John F. Witte, professor of political science at the University of Wisconsin, has explored parents' satisfaction with the private schools their children were attending. On every measure—from parental involvement to school discipline—their satisfaction level was high.

In short, parents and students seem overwhelmingly pleased with their chosen schools. The convenience of location may be a factor. The safer, more supportive environment of the school may be important. Mary E. Driscoll of New York University offers another possible ex-planation: The very act of choosing, and being chosen, may itself en-gender satisfaction, since it gives the enterprise an air of selectivity.[9] Regardless of the reasons, those participating in school choice generally feel good about the decisions they have made.

> *Sixth, the educational impact of school choice is ambiguous at best. In some districtwide programs, a correlation may ex-ist between choice and the improvement of students' aca-demic performance. In statewide programs, no such connec-tion could be found.*

At the heart of school choice is the expectation that a competitive market system will benefit participating students educationally and bring academic vitality to the nation's public schools. However, we found little evidence to support such a position in statewide choice programs. Indeed, none of the thirteen states with open enrollment has yet demonstrated significant educational gains attributable to choice.

Results are more encouraging in selected districtwide programs. Even here, though, the academic impact of school choice is unclear. Students in Cambridge, Massachusetts, and Montclair, New Jersey, for example, perform quite well on standardized tests in the basics and have made gains in recent years. It is possible, we believe, to attribute these achievements at least in part to the revitalizing influence of school choice and to active parent participation. However, these districts have, through the years, been relatively well-funded. It is therefore difficult to determine to what extent choice, in and of itself, is responsible for such improvement. Further, in both districts, minority and poor students still trail their white counterparts on every measure. Still, the overall achievement of these "choice" districts is impressive.

East Harlem presents perhaps the most fascinating picture. When the district opened its first alternative school eighteen years ago, it ranked near the bottom in the city. Choice seemed to energize East Harlem schools, freeing them from bureaucratic constraints, giving parents and students more clearly defined alternatives, and enabling teachers to develop creative new ideas. In this enlivened climate, educational gains were achieved. Test scores improved, moving the district from thirty-first in the city in 1973 to fifteenth in 1982. Further, the number of East Harlem students accepted at some of the city's most competitive public high schools rose from fewer than twenty in 1973 to more than three hundred today.

In recent years, however, academic performance in East Harlem has leveled off, even declining on some measures. In 1992, only 38 percent of the students in that district scored at or above grade level on standardized reading tests. And East Harlem now ranks twenty-second out of the city's thirty-two districts (table 8). We do not discount the progress made. East Harlem has made great gains, attributable at least in part to choice. And we surely do not mean to suggest that test scores are the only way to measure progress. Rather, the point is that a careful review of the most recent evidence shows that, despite the gains, East Harlem still confronts serious problems. Choice is not enough.

Table 8

District 4 Rank Among Thirty-two New York City Districts
*(Based on Reading Scores, Grades Two Through Nine,*
*1972–73 to 1991–92)*

| YEAR | RANK |
|------|------|
| 1972–73 | 31 |
| 1973–74 | 32 |
| 1974–75 | 29 |
| 1975–76 | 27 |
| 1976–77 | NA |
| 1977–78 | 28 |
| 1978–79 | NA |
| 1979–80 | 22 |
| 1980–81 | 17 |
| 1981–82 | 15 |
| 1982–83 | 17 |
| 1983–84 | 17 |
| 1984–85 | 18 |
| 1985–86 | 18 |
| 1986–87 | 17 |
| 1987–88 | 19 |
| 1988–89 | 21 |
| 1989–90 | 21 |
| 1990–91 | 21 |
| 1991–92 | 22 |

NA: Not available.
SOURCE: Calculations by The Carnegie Foundation for the Advancement of Teaching based on test data from the New York City Board of Education.

Finally, in weighing the impact of school choice on educational quality, and most especially on school renewal, we cite a recent national study that compared sixty-six ''choice'' schools (schools chosen by students and parents) around the country with a matched sample of ''nonchoice'' schools. The study reported ''no significant difference'' between these two groups in content of curriculum, time spent on different kinds of instructional activities, amount of homework assigned, school organization, extracurricular activities, or the experience and educational levels of teachers.[10]

Lauren A. Sosniak, of Washington University in St. Louis, and Corinna A. Ethington, of the University of Illinois at Chicago, who wrote this study, offered several observations about these findings. "On the one hand," they said, "we may argue that public schools of choice are not yet living up to their promise for educational innovation. Perhaps choice programs have not been implemented appropriately or perhaps they have not yet had sufficient time to develop innovative curricula. Or perhaps school and district administrators have discovered that what the choice parents and students want has little to do with innovative curricula. . . . On the other hand, we may argue that the typical *non-choice schools* are not as standardized as critics have led us to believe, and that these schools have more potential for educational innovation than we typically assume."[11]

What we have, then, is a mixed report card on the relationship between school choice and school improvement. While educational gains have been made in selected districts, it seems clear that other factors besides choice have been involved. Further, as far as we have been able to determine, the impact of statewide programs has been marginal at best. We conclude that a competitive model alone will not lift the educational performance of the nation's schools.

*Seventh, school choice, to be successful, requires significant administrative and financial support. It is not a cheap path to educational reform.*

In the school choice debate, the matter of money is rarely thoughtfully discussed. The assumption seems to be that choice will require few if any additional dollars and may, in fact, reduce costs through competition and increased efficiency. This is a major miscalculation. In every districtwide program we examined, significant additional administrative and financial support has been crucial. A recent U.S. Department of Education report states the case precisely: "There are certain costs for public school choice programs which are specific to them and which can be separated for school improvement." These include, the report says, costs for planning time, information gathering, outreach, training, and transportation.[12]

Cambridge, Massachusetts, illustrates the point. It is one of the nation's most celebrated "choice" districts. It also happens to be near

23

the top in the state in per-student expenditures, at $9,200 in 1992–93. Further, Cambridge has been unusually successful in attracting outside grants as well as support services from industry and from the distinguished academic institutions that surround it. This high level of funding is, of course, not linked directly to school choice. Still, in weighing Cambridge's successes, it's important to bear in mind that the choice program is undergirded by a solid financial base.

Montclair, which has another successful program, is also a well-funded district—spending $7,478 per student in 1992. It also has, through the years, received millions of dollars in state and federal desegregation funds to create distinctive magnet schools and train teachers. As for East Harlem, officials told us that during the 1970s and 1980s the district received more federal money per pupil than any in the nation to help build its network of twenty-nine alternative middle schools. The point is clear: choice costs.

In implementing choice, money is needed for a variety of reasons, but transportation costs are especially significant. Since parents in the same neighborhood may send their children to different schools, traditional bus routes will no longer work. As a result, many districts with "choice" programs have had to expand bus routes, run double shifts, or even hire fleets of taxis. In Kansas City, Missouri, which has a modified program, the district uses up to four hundred taxicabs to transport students from home to school.[13]

In Montclair, transportation expenditures have increased by approximately $1.5 million annually as a result of the "choice" program. In Cambridge, 15 percent of the students rode school buses in 1981— the year before school choice was introduced. Now, 64 percent ride buses to get to school. As a result, transportation costs in that district rose from $183,000 in 1981–82 to $407,000 a decade later (table 9). Much of this increase reflected the added commitments imposed by choice. In St. Paul, school officials estimate that the average annual cost of transporting students who attend neighborhood schools is $120 per student. For students attending non-neighborhood "choice" schools, the average cost nearly triples, to $350.

The U.S. Department of Education, in its recent school choice report, concludes that "safe, efficient transportation for students is essen-

24

Table 9

School Transportation Expenditures in Cambridge
*(1978–79 to 1991–92)*

| FISCAL YEAR | EXPENDITURE |
|---|---|
| 1978–79 | $126,300 |
| 1980–81 | 172,577 |
| 1981–82* | 182,580 |
| 1984–85 | 298,931 |
| 1989–90 | 476,220 |
| 1991–92** | 407,378 |

\* Districtwide choice plan went into effect.
\*\* Starting times for bus routes were staggered.
*Note*: Forty-one percent of the district's transportation expenditures are reimbursed by the state under school desegregation regulations.
SOURCE: Cambridge Public Schools annual budgets.

tial to the success and fairness of public school choice. . . . Unfortunately, transportation also can be a limiting factor. It is costly and complicated, and some "choice" programs have had to compromise on what would be the most desirable system in order to stay within financial limits or a reasonable travel distance."[14]

We do not suggest that money invested in school choice is misplaced. We do insist, however, that if choice is to work, added expenditures are required.

*Eighth, statewide "choice" programs tend to widen the gap between rich and poor districts.*

School choice is built on the marketplace model, yet often overlooked is the fact that schools vary greatly in their *capacity* to compete. In almost every state, local school resources differ dramatically from one district to another. Consider Nebraska, a state where school choice has been adopted. In 1990–91, per-pupil spending in that state ranged from $2,985 in one district to $10,534 in another. In Massachusetts, another "choice" state, per-student expenditures across districts ranged from $2,817 to $8,634. And across the nation there are many other examples of such discrepancies (table 10).

Table 10

School District Spending in Thirteen
States with Statewide Choice Programs
*(1989–90 and 1990–91)*

| | PER-STUDENT EXPENDITURES IN LOWEST AND HIGHEST SPENDING DISTRICTS | |
| | LOWEST | HIGHEST |
| --- | --- | --- |
| Alabama | $2,656 | $ 4,773 |
| Arkansas | 2,081 | 5,843 |
| California* | 2,692 | 11,740 |
| Colorado | 3,740 | 13,617 |
| Idaho | 2,133 | 7,806 |
| Iowa* | 3,668 | 7,478 |
| Massachusetts | 2,817 | 8,634 |
| Michigan | 2,491 | 8,407 |
| Minnesota* | 3,470 | 10,200 |
| Nebraska | 2,985 | 10,534 |
| Oregon* | 2,953 | 10,350 |
| Utah* | 2,504 | 10,252 |
| Washington | 3,375 | 14,229 |

* 1990–91 figures; others are for 1989–90.
SOURCE: *Education Week*, Vol. 11, No. 39, 17 June 1992, p. 28.

Money alone does not ensure excellence in education. But neither can the need for resources be casually dismissed. Time and time again we observed that in the districts with the lowest levels of spending, facilities are less adequate, teachers are less well paid, textbooks are outdated, and library and laboratory equipment are shockingly insufficient. Clearly, when poor districts are forced to vie with wealthier ones for students and dollars, they are placed in a bidding war they cannot win.

The impact of this uneven playing field was vividly revealed in Massachusetts. Brockton, a nearly bankrupt city south of Boston, spent less than $5,000 per pupil in 1991–92. In recent years the district has laid off scores of teachers and increased class sizes due to chronic fiscal problems. Avon, its far smaller suburban neighbor, spent twice as much per high school pupil—$10,239. Avon's school library boasts twenty-five sets of encyclopedias. The district has late-model computers, microfiche equipment, and satellite dishes connecting students to class-rooms around the world and linking teachers to training programs. Its high school has a home economics lab, a photo lab, an art studio, a woodshop, physics and chemistry labs, a professionally equipped cable television studio, and three kitchens.

The one thing Avon needed was more students and, under the re-cently instituted statewide choice plan, it got them at Brockton's ex-pense. During the first year, 135 Brockton students moved to Avon, taking with them nearly one million dollars in state aid. Further, Brock-ton had to *pay* Avon additional money just to match the affluent dis-trict's higher per-student cost. Brockton, with fewer resources, simply could not compete with its richer neighbor. The gap widened between the privileged and the disadvantaged.

Brockton may be one of the nation's biggest losers under choice. But we found others. Exira is a relatively poor district in south-central Iowa, with 374 students. It was forced to raise local taxes sharply to make up for the sudden loss of forty students and $140,000 in state aid out of its $2 million school budget to Audubon, its larger, more affluent neighbor just ten miles away. Are Avon, Massachusetts, and Audubon, Iowa, winning the choice contest because they are pushing back the frontiers of school reform? Or are they winning because they have more resources? Undeniably, the relative wealth of districts is a crucial factor when it comes to competing in a school choice program.

*Ninth, school choice works best when it is arrived at gradu-ally, locally, and voluntarily—not by top-down mandates.*

When choice programs are imposed on all districts by state legis-lative mandate, they are least successful. Yet, in many states, that is exactly what's going on. Choice laws have been enacted without thoughtful deliberation or public comment. As a result, parents and cit-izens are left largely in the dark. School boards have little opportunity to anticipate the impact. Teachers and administrators have little or no time for creative planning. This top-down strategy explains, at least in part, why most statewide choice programs have been singularly unsuc-cessful.

27

In contrast, the best "choice" programs we observed were in single districts like Cambridge, East Harlem, and Montclair, where the plans evolved gradually. No districtwide referendum was involved. Still, parents were engaged at every stage, through living-room discussions and public meetings that brought the community together. Parents in these districts were given many options from which to choose, transportation was available to students, and the funding level from school to school was more equitable than in statewide programs. Further, in all of these districts, active parent participation was ongoing—and this, we believe, is one of the greatest benefits of school choice.

We conclude this review of our findings on a cautionary note. On the one hand, we were impressed that selected districts have been revitalized by choice programs. Time and time again, we heard from participating parents and students about how pleased they are with the programs selected.

At the same time, we discovered that most parents support the neighborhood schools and are not inclined to transfer their children to another school. Further, in states where choice has been introduced, participation is minimal, and those parents who do select another school often base their decisions on convenience factors rather than academic concerns. In addition, we observed that when wealthy schools and poor ones are asked to compete, the gap between the privileged and the disadvantaged widens—and children often are the losers. In summary, while school choice has a vital role to play, it seems unrealistic to expect that choice alone will renew the nation's schools.

# CHAPTER 3

## *Districtwide Choice: Montclair, Cambridge, East Harlem*

E AST HARLEM in New York City, along with Cambridge, Massachusetts, and Montclair, New Jersey, are the nation's "stars of choice." These districts are routinely cited as evidence that school choice can indeed deliver excellence to all, including children in the most challenging environments. Even education leaders who generally are skeptical of choice's potential have hailed these places for their efforts.

East Harlem's Community School District 4 serves one of New York City's poorest neighborhoods. In 1973, when the process leading to choice began, it ranked near the bottom in the city on virtually every educational measure. Cambridge is a district that enrolls the offspring of Harvard and M.I.T. professors, struggling black and Hispanic families, and immigrants speaking Portuguese and more than forty other languages. Cambridge became a pioneer in 1981 when it adopted choice as a strategy to achieve racial integration. Montclair, New Jersey, a sophisticated, racially and economically diverse suburb near New York City, introduced choice in the mid-1970s as "white flight" threatened. Today, the district's extensive system of choice has students from million-dollar homes attending classes side-by-side with children poor enough to qualify for free lunches.

Even in these districts, choice has its limits. In all three, parents and students are asked to list several school preferences within their district, but nowhere is their first request guaranteed. In Montclair and Cambridge, choice is restricted by available space and the requirement for racial balance. In East Harlem, the schools have greater freedom to select their students, but the local board also plays referee to assure that

29

no program grows too "elitist" by skimming off the most gifted, most motivated, best-behaved students.

Hundreds of districts around the country operate "choice" programs of one sort or another, with magnet schools or various specialty programs for selected students. Some of these programs existed long before the debate over school choice began. But several important conditions set Montclair, Cambridge, and especially East Harlem apart.

First, all three have virtually done away with neighborhood-school zoning at particular grade levels—in effect, *requiring* parents of students at particular grade levels to become active school choosers. Second, each has moved beyond the goal of desegregation and designed a "choice" system to promote cooperation and school betterment throughout the entire district. Third, choice in all three districts was born from a long, painstaking, grassroots process. We visited each of these places to understand better both the strengths and limitations of school choice at the district level.

## Montclair, New Jersey

Edgemont Montessori School. Bradford Academy. Mt. Hebron School. They sound like posh private schools. In fact, they are among the eight elementary magnet schools, two middle schools, and one high school that comprise Montclair's much-heralded "choice" program.

Montclair's plan was designed to meet three goals: to voluntarily integrate schools, diversify programs, and raise student achievement. To a considerable degree, this 5,400-pupil suburban district has succeeded in achieving these objectives. The racial balance in all "choice" schools is close to fifty-fifty.[1] Districtwide student performance is encouraging, and the programs are unusually diverse. They include a science and technology magnet school, a Montessori school, a school that emphasizes communication skills, an international program based on foreign-language study, two "gifted and talented" schools, and a new "family magnet" for pre-kindergarten through second grade which focuses on family involvement in early education.

The differences among schools go beyond subject themes to learning and teaching styles. Parents who choose Bradford Academy, for

30

example, find an intimate, traditionally structured environment for pre-schoolers through fifth-graders. But Hillside Elementary offers third-, fourth-, and fifth-graders more than 250 electives from which to choose. Montclair superintendent Dr. Mary Lee Fitzgerald says, ''Hillside asks seven-, eight-, and nine-year-olds to schedule themselves like college students. Some kids would be lost in that situation. So we work a great deal with parents to help them understand the learning style of their kids, and try to find the right match in the school. We also ask, what does your family value? If you value a lot of homework, text-books, tests, go with it.'' Fitzgerald adds: ''We have schools that are geared toward the style of the learners.''

School choice did not come to Montclair because its schools were failing. This has always been a high achieving district with highly mo-tivated parents. Rather, the events leading up to choice date to the late 1960s, when Montclair was ordered to desegregate.[2] According to long-time residents, tensions ran high. Crosses were burned. Real es-tate values fell. Racial unrest in neighboring Newark and East Orange intensified fears that many residents would abandon the public schools. Even the most open-minded citizens insisted that they would not sacri-fice their children to strife-torn schools.

A forced-busing plan in the early 1970s led to significant ''white flight'' and even more racial imbalance. Then, in 1976, Montclair pro-posed, and the state approved, one of the nation's earliest ''choice'' plans aimed at achieving voluntary desegregation. The district opened a gifted program in a minority neighborhood, hoping it would attract whites. A ''traditional'' program stressing basics was established in a predominantly white neighborhood, in hopes of attracting blacks.[3] The district provided transportation for all students beyond walking dis-tance.[4] Still, declines in the white student population continued, and in 1984 the district's delicate racial balance was, once again, threatened.

Montclair then moved to its present comprehensive plan, doing away with all school boundaries and transforming all elementary schools into magnet programs with distinctive curricular themes. The plan's underlying philosophy is that no school is right for every child, or for that matter every teacher. The belief is that if choice is to lead to true diversity and excellence, then schools must be willing to tell parents or even teachers that a particular school just might not be the best place for them.

Watchung School, for example, a science and technology magnet school, lacks lavishly appointed labs. The school demands from its teachers, however, that they develop a high level of technical and scientific knowledge. As part of Watchung's transition from neighborhood school to science magnet, teachers were paid to participate in a two-week summer training program at Bank Street College of Education, and Bank Street experts came every other week during the school year to work with teachers. Principal Barbara Strobert says she loses about two teachers a year because they can't, or won't, adjust to that kind of demand. "People who come into this building have to understand this," said fifth-grade teacher Edward O'Connor.

Under the current Montclair plan, all parents are required to list two choices from among the district's eight elementary schools. More than 90 percent get one of their preferences, again dictated mainly by available space and the imperative of racial balance. No "choice" school in Montclair, not even those for the gifted and talented, has academic admissions criteria.

At Hillside Elementary, one such magnet, teachers are trained in the belief that all children have a gift; it's up to the school to discover and nurture it. Seventy-six of the 640 students, in fact, have disabilities that qualify them for special education. One student who has a significant neurological impairment illustrates Hillside's approach. The boy's father told principal Michael J. Chiles that his son seemed to "come alive" at football games when the crowd cheered and applauded. "We wondered if he would respond positively to drama. Sure enough, he gets on stage, and he's transformed. He played Martin Luther King in our school play this year, and he had to memorize three of his speeches. His talent might never have been picked up otherwise," said Chiles.

While many parents are pleased that they have the right to choose their children's schools, some told us that it's difficult, almost unreasonably so, to decide for their young ones, whose abilities and learning styles are still evolving. To help parents select the right schools for their children, the district must give parents information about their options, and informing parents is, indeed, one of Montclair's greatest strengths. All elementary schools in the district offer parents tours during February and March. Roughly three-quarters of the parents participate, and some parents actually show up with minicams.[5] Brochures describing each program are distributed, and many schools issue weekly bulletins. Parents, of course, also depend on each other for information. One survey found that for as many as 89 percent, the most prevalent way of gathering information was "talking to others."[6] As a result of these efforts, most parents we interviewed seemed to be educated "consumers."

What can we learn from Montclair? Importantly, while the initial moves were spurred by desegregation mandates, choice in that district did evolve gradually out of discussions among parents, teachers, and administrators. The resulting system of magnet schools offers almost uniformly desirable options. Principals and teachers say competition among programs "keeps them on their toes," and it is clear that the program encourages a strong entrepreneurial spirit among educators. We were told by school principals, however, that this doesn't always promote cooperation. "Good educational ideas," said one, "are guarded as jealously as industrial secrets." Another principal said, "We don't do a lot of sharing, principal to principal. If I'm doing something great, the success story is sent around the district. But we don't tell each other in advance. Principals burn out quick here," he added.

Further, Montclair illustrates that choice is not cost-free. The district has a firm commitment to provide the resources needed to shore up weak programs and maintain strong ones—and that takes money. And although Montclair's compact size helps keep down some extra costs, such as for transportation and parent information, the need for substantial additional money cannot be avoided. For example, the district buses about half its children daily because of choice—far more than the 10 to 15 percent typical in the state—and therefore, choice adds about $1.5 million each year to Montclair's transportation costs, according to district officials.

The district has enjoyed a solid funding base—$7,478 per student—but that has been somewhat eroded. In addition, Montclair has, until very recently, received from $1.5 to $2.5 million annually in state and federal desegregation funds, making possible the special equipment and teacher training needed for distinctive magnet programs. But the district lost its desegregation funding this year, which forced it to reduce summer programs and encourage early teacher retirements.

Bringing excellence to all students, regardless of race, ethnicity, or economic circumstance, has been Montclair's toughest challenge. Overall, students in grades two through eight averaged in the 84th to 95th percentile in reading and math on the Iowa Test of Basic Skills in the spring of 1991. But the test scores of minority students still lag. In 1988, the district established an Office of Minority Achievement to confront this problem and raise consciousness in every school. One encouraging signal: twelve out of seventy of the district's National Honor Society award recipients last year were minority students, up from just one three years earlier, says Chandler Dennis, head of the office. The percentage of Montclair's nonwhites accepted at four-year colleges is also up, from 50 percent before 1988 to 59 percent in June 1991—but well below the 82 percent of white students accepted.

Dennis believes, however, that strong leadership from the top, not choice, has been the key in the gains by minority students: "I don't see a direct correlation between choice and increased achievement." Indeed, Montclair's other administrators stress that success has stemmed from many factors, not just choice.

School choice, then, has not solved all of Montclair's problems. Still, from what we've observed, it has helped promote racial integration and brought a sense of energy to the district. At the same time, the town's compact geography; highly educated, relatively affluent, and open-minded parents; committed school leaders and teachers; and not least, bountiful state and federal funding have all been crucial to success. As one longtime resident put it: "Montclair is a very unusual town. Whatever happens here, it's hard to compare it. You have to look at the kinds of people who choose to be here. You have an incredibly urbane, educated population which demands excellent schools but isn't afraid to integrate."

## CAMBRIDGE, MASSACHUSETTS

Just a ten-minute drive separates the bookstores of Brattle Street in Harvard Square from the bodegas of the multilingual neighborhoods of East

34

Cambridge. As close as they are in miles, these communities are worlds apart, and so are the children who live and learn in them. Cambridge's public schools must educate the privileged offspring of professors along with those of the poor and working class populations in this city of a hundred thousand across the Charles River from Boston.

Since 1981, Cambridge has operated a ''choice'' plan aimed at achieving integration and bringing excellence to all children. As with Montclair, choice in Cambridge evolved gradually. In the early 1970s, the district decided to head off a possible state desegregation order due to racial imbalance at several schools. In response, each school formed a desegregation committee consisting of parents, teachers, and others in the community. They, in turn, were represented on a citywide committee.

When the resulting open enrollment program was first introduced in Cambridge, the district did not provide transportation for students who selected schools outside their neighborhoods, so the plan had few takers. What followed was a more comprehensive grassroots effort consisting of community meetings, school mergers, and redrawn neighborhood school lines, all aimed at attracting parents into the planning process. Ten years later, on March 3, 1981, the current plan was enacted, ending neighborhood zoning and providing transportation to all students needing it.

That fall, news camera crews crowded into Cambridge expecting violence as the first buses rolled students to their new schools. But a decade of careful planning and community participation paid off: buses came and went without incident. With the help of the Harvard Graduate School of Education, schools with different ethnic mixes were combined and transformed. ''What evolved was a process of getting people together and instilling the notion of ownership in what eventually became the Cambridge Controlled Choice Plan,'' said Bert Giroux, the district's long-time public information officer.

In Cambridge, choice proved to be an important catalyst for the change, says superintendent Mary Lou McGrath: ''I think it had a tremendous influence. Everybody started talking about education. Some teachers had to pay a little more attention. Teachers began realizing we have customers.'' And these customers seem to be pleased. One survey found that 83 percent of parents rate Cambridge's schools as either very good or good, while only 3 percent give them a poor grade.[7]

When it comes to choice's impact on student performance, the picture is less clear. Scores on standardized tests reveal academic progress in some areas, but problems in others. The district reports that, compared to national norms, its students have relatively high scores in eighth-grade math, reading, social studies, and science; lower scores in fourth-grade basic skills; and still lower scores in twelfth grade. In 1991, 76 percent of Cambridge's third-, sixth-, and ninth-graders passed the reading, math, and writing sections of the Massachusetts Basic Skills Test, up from 62 percent in 1987. Scholastic Aptitude Test scores rose by 89 points from 1981 to 1988, to a combined 859, but in 1991 sank back to 805—91 points below the national average.

All fourteen of Cambridge's magnet schools, covering kindergarten through grade eight, have achieved racial balance. Yet, poor, immigrant, non-English speakers remain relatively isolated in one or two schools, and minority students are generally overrepresented in special education and underrepresented in honors programs. Indeed, one-fourth of the district's students are in special education, while the state average is about 15 percent and the national average is about 10 percent. An estimated three-fourths of Cambridge's special education students are minority or poor; many have no discernible handicap but simply lag in basic skills.

At the Harrington School, located in a working class section of East Cambridge several miles from Harvard Yard, 446 of the school's 700 children in kindergarten through eighth grade speak a language other than English as their native tongue. Many choose this school because they feel more comfortable in their own neighborhood. This means, however, that standardized test scores in reading and math are consistently lower for third- and sixth-graders at Harrington than those, say, at Peabody School, where only 20 of the 435 students are non-English speakers. What passes for a science lab at Harrington is little more than a cabinet and sink. In contrast, Peabody's science program has strong ties to the Massachusetts Institute of Technology, and students hear talks by top scientists like the chief engineer of the space shuttle program.

36

In examining school choice in Cambridge, money must once again be considered. Cambridge is one of the state's top-spending districts, reaching $9,200 per pupil in 1992–93, almost double the state average. Further, the district has received, throughout the years, millions of dollars in state desegregation funds, which have helped support magnet programs, subsidize transportation, and train teachers. In addition, Cambridge was one of the few districts where voters decided to override Massachusetts Proposition 2½, enacted a decade ago to limit property tax increases.

In Cambridge, as in Montclair, transportation costs have increased because of choice. In 1980–81, the year before choice was introduced, only 15 percent of the district's elementary school children rode school buses, at a cost of $172,577. In 1989–90, 64 percent of the students attended magnet schools outside their immediate neighborhood, and transportation costs rose to $476,220. They dipped to $407,378 in 1991–92 after the district staggered pickup times on bus routes. Fortunately, the state pays 41 percent of Cambridge's busing costs with desegregation funds.

Cambridge also has invested $65,000 in its effective parent information program. This center keeps parents informed of their educational options—in six different languages. Most parents have, in fact, become informed consumers. They place the highest value on good teachers, academic reputation, and security in making their school selection. Two out of three Cambridge parents actually visit schools while choosing, indicating a fairly high level of involvement.[8] One further measure of outreach: twenty-one homeless families have been brought into the schools. Indeed, Cambridge's parent information program has received wide acclaim and is being imitated by other Massachusetts cities, including Boston.

Because of a solid funding base, Cambridge is one of the rare Massachusetts districts to have avoided heavy teacher layoffs during the recession, enabling it to attract and keep a capable teaching force. Over 90 percent of parents think their children's teachers are truly committed and respect their children as individuals, according to one survey.[9] Added resources have, in fact, led to staffing increases in the district, including a student assignment officer, a citywide parent coordinator, a clerk, thirteen school-assigned parent tour guides, and 256 full- and part-time aides, at a total additional expense of $788,000.

Finally, choice has forced Cambridge to develop an extraordinarily high level of accountability. The district now employs an elaborate budgeting process to assure that each "choice" school gets its fair share of resources. The result is a three-inch thick budget document more like that of a multi-billion dollar conglomerate than a school system spending $71 million. The district has employed an executive director for financial review and a budget manager with a staff of four. It also operates a $72,000 grant administration office which has easily paid for itself by attracting some $3.2 million in government and private grants.

Cambridge superintendent McGrath says: "When I go around the country, I tell people that you have to provide the choices, and that's expensive. You have to provide the support services. And every parent needs information, and transportation. That's equity, and that's fairness." She concludes: "You can't have choice unless you're willing to pay." Clearly, the myth that choice offers a cheap, easy path to national school reform dies in Cambridge.

Again choice has not been an educational cure-all for Cambridge. Still, it is certainly one of several key factors that have helped move the district into the front ranks of America's most reform-minded urban districts.


EAST HARLEM, NEW YORK CITY

Monday, October 16, 1989 was to be an evening of triumph for East Harlem.

Seated on the auditorium stage of Intermediate School 117 was then-U.S. Secretary of Education Lauro Cavazos, flanked by the education commissioner of New York State and other local officials. A few months earlier, President Bush had called school choice "the single most promising idea" in the reform movement, and Cavazos had come to pay homage to this impoverished upper Manhattan district, which the White House and other champions of choice had repeatedly praised as the promise fulfilled. Yet for two and one half hours, East Harlem parents and community activists made clear to the visiting delegation

38

from Washington that their schools needed more than choice. "The irony is that we are here celebrating choice at a time when we're in a crisis in this district," said Ray Rivera, the father of two children attending East Harlem public schools. "Instead of increased support, we're getting less."[10]

We found that many East Harlem residents view as a mixed blessing the national acclaim showered on their schools since the district adopted its revolutionary system a decade ago. On the one hand, there is justified pride in the accomplishments of choice and the fame it has brought. "If there is a single district that deserves to be held up as a model for all the others," say champions of choice Chubb and Moe, "it is East Harlem."[11] But there's concern, too, that such praise has distorted both the extent of the district's educational accomplishments and choice's true role in achieving them. It's as if the nation has been asked to believe that generations of distress in one of America's most blighted communities—where eight out of ten students are poor enough to qualify for free lunch, 10 percent don't speak English, and the median family income is under $9,000—have been erased in a single stroke by "choice."

District 4 was a propitious site for choice. It serves some thirteen thousand children, is a compact 2.2 square miles, and has all the mass transit needed to whisk students from one school to another. Further, declining enrollment from the 1970s through the mid-1980s meant that there was plenty of room in existing schools for new programs and new students. During those years, the district replaced its thirteen overcrowded middle schools with twenty-nine alternative programs, each with about two hundred or fewer students.

For East Harlem residents, the choice process starts formally during the fifth or sixth grade as students move from elementary schools to one of the district's alternative schools. It resembles, in many ways, the admissions process at private schools. Parents receive an information booklet in the fall with brief descriptions of each program. They are urged to attend orientation sessions to get more details. Sixth-grade teachers advise parents and students on how to make wise choices, and students then complete an application listing up to six selections.

East Harlem's "choice" process differs crucially from Montclair's or Cambridge's. In this district, admissions decisions are made in large part by the schools themselves, not by the central school board. This is possible because choice came to East Harlem not out of pressure to integrate but out of the district's desire to innovate and improve quality. Further, there is a strong philosophic belief in the district that program diversity can only be achieved if each school is given a high level of control over its programs and admissions policies.

Each of East Harlem's schools has three weeks to choose from among the students who have selected it as first preference. Applicants rejected in the first round are then sent to the second-choice school, and so on, for three rounds. More than 90 percent get one of their first three selections, district officials say. The remaining students are assigned by the local board to other schools.

The application form in East Harlem requests standardized test scores and asks sixth-grade teachers to rate the pupil's work habits, attendance record, and academic abilities, all on a scale of one to five. These more objective criteria until recently were combined with highly subjective judgments. Early application forms even asked teachers to rate a child "as a person," but the district eliminated that category in 1992.

What's most distinctive about the East Harlem plan is that teachers are given great autonomy in shaping the educational program at each school. At East Harlem Tech, for example, social studies teacher Perla Wander took the lead in launching an elaborate project in which students drafted a school constitution, conducted a community voter drive, wrote a school anthem, held a presidential debate, and established a social studies museum. "We have freedom from administration," Wander said. "We come up with an idea, and they let us develop it."

Junior High School 99 exemplifies these positive changes. Ed Rodriguez, outgoing principal, recalls that the building used to be packed with three thousand students and was rife with violence and gang activity. Today, violence is rare. The building now houses five alternative programs, including Manhattan East—a school so well regarded, it draws middle-class students from around the city. "Today there are 840 kids in this building. There are five directors, and they know every kid in their program,'' Rodriguez said.

Yet, as with Montclair and Cambridge, it's nearly impossible to pinpoint choice's role in bringing about progress in East Harlem. From what we have learned, three factors in addition to choice were critically important: an extraordinary group of school leaders, administrators, and teachers; large infusions of federal, local, and private funds; and a decision to break down large, impersonal middle schools into smaller, more caring places.

The importance of thoughtful leadership from teachers and administrators cannot be overstated. During the 1970s and early 1980s, District 4 discovered a powerful lineup of school reformers in its own ranks. Seymour Fliegel was the district's first director of alternative programs and later its deputy superintendent. Fliegel believed that the best way to change a problem-plagued district was not by edicts from the board but school by school. He also wisely acknowledged that teachers themselves were a key source of innovation. Fliegel recalls how junior-high teacher Mike Friedman approached him with a proposal to establish a new ''Bridge School'' for tough-to-teach middle school kids. ''Friedman comes to me and says, 'I like hoods. I'm not going to treat them like hoods.' Suddenly what you learn is that there are smart hoods. Bridge School really makes citizens out of those kids,'' recalls Fliegel. ''The magic of District 4,'' he says, ''was that you had this hero effect, people who developed single marvelous schools. But the whole district turned around because there was a culture to protect each school. We institutionalized change.''

In 1974, Deborah Meier opened Central Park East, the district's first, and arguably best, alternative school. The former kindergarten teacher, now recognized as one of America's premier urban educators, helped set the pattern for what followed in subsequent alternative schools. She insisted that parents choose her school rather than simply being assigned to it, kept her school small, and drew on the learner-centered philosophies of Theodore Sizer, head of the Coalition of Essential Schools.

Leading it all was Anthony Alvarado. Named district superintendent in 1972, the former teacher had an unrivalled capacity to bend rules, attract outside grants, cajole an often hostile city bureaucracy, and woo the powerful teacher and principal unions to create and nurture small, distinctive programs. Alvarado's initiatives, aimed at boosting reading scores and bilingual programs, lifted District 4's profile and vaulted him to a brief term as New York City's school chancellor in 1982.[12] "I put choice in because you can give poorer people more options," Alvarado now says. "It created a little sense of competition. A junior high school teacher told me that in twenty-six years he'd never visited another school in the district until choice. So choice helps break down professional isolation. It stirs the pot. But leadership," Alvarado stresses, "was significantly more important than choice."

Again, though, as in Montclair and Cambridge, money played a central role in District 4. From the 1970s through the mid-1980s, the district received, we were told by one official, more federal money per student than any in the nation, and for years it exceeded its budget by 3 to 5 percent each year.[13] Further, from 1984 to 1988, the district received about $1.5 million per year in federal magnet grants, enabling it to hire approximately thirty extra teachers to help carry out its unusually small programs. The district's bid for a continuation of those federal funds was denied in 1989—clearly dampening the enthusiasm with which Harlem residents greeted Cavazos' visit that year.

In the last five years, East Harlem has had the same acute money woes encountered by all local boards in New York City. Tight money has slowed the pace of innovation and forced the district into difficult trade-offs: fewer books, supplies, field trips, and enrichment activities in order to keep programs small. The fiscal problems "have meant losing good teachers who have left for Nassau and Westchester counties," said Friedman, director of the Bridge School. "I lost three key teachers, including my most experienced math and science teacher."

But what about the students? Despite current problems, most students we spoke with have positive attitudes towards their schools. During our interviews in a dozen alternative schools, students told us they felt safer, were proud of their schools, and welcomed the intimacy of the smaller programs: "We're all like family," said an eighth-grader at East Harlem Tech.

As for academic progress in East Harlem, it's most frequently noted that the number of East Harlem elementary students accepted at New York City's top high schools rose from fewer than twenty in 1973 to more than three hundred today. The Heritage Foundation has also declared that choice has raised East Harlem's average reading scores to "over 65 percent today," moving the district from dead last in New York City to "17th out of 32 districts. . . ."[14]

The problem is that these test data are not up-to-date and are accordingly misleading. East Harlem's 1991–92 standardized reading scores are, in fact, nearly 27 percentage points lower than those cited, and its rank last year among New York City's thirty-two local school districts was twenty-second, not seventeenth. In 1991–92, 38.3 percent of District 4's students in grades two through nine scored at or above grade level in reading, 8.1 percentage points below the citywide average (table 11). That was 3.7 percentage points below the previous year. The citywide drop was 2.8 percent.[15]

In math, District 4 students in grades two through eight ranked twenty-third out of thirty-two city districts in 1991–92. This reflected a slight improvement in its relative standing from the previous year, when it ranked twenty-sixth. In 1991–92, 48.7 percent of East Harlem's students scored at or above grade level, a drop of 1.7 percentage points from a year earlier, and below the citywide average of 58.4 percent.[16]

Further, we found sharp disparities among District 4's "choice" programs. In 1990–91 in ten of the programs, at least half the students scored at or above grade level on standardized math and reading tests. In three middle schools, 90 percent of the students scored at or above grade level. At four other schools, fewer than one of every ten students managed to score at or above grade level in math.[17]

Clearly, then, when it comes to student achievement, serious problems remain.

District 4 officials argue, justifiably we believe, that standardized test scores by themselves are not a barometer of school quality. "There is no hard measure," said the head of one school where fewer than 40 percent are at grade level in reading. "If you look at kids who are testing in the third percentile in reading, they're not going to be in the fiftieth percentile in a year or two. We look for steady growth. We're

## Table 11

### Percentage of Students in Grades Two through Nine
### Reading at or above Grade Level in New York City and District 4
*(1972–73 to 1991–92)*

| YEAR | NEW YORK CITY | DISTRICT 4 |
|---|---|---|
| 1972–73[1] | 34.0% | 15.9% |
| 1973–74 | 33.8 | 15.3 |
| 1974–75[2] | 45.2 | 28.3 |
| 1975–76 | 42.6 | 27.9 |
| 1976–77[3] | 40.1 | 29.7 |
| 1977–78 | 43.0 | 25.9 |
| 1978–79 | 40.3 | 25.9 |
| 1979–80 | 46.7 | 35.6 |
| 1980–81 | 50.8 | 44.3 |
| 1981–82[4] | 51.0 | 48.5 |
| 1982–83 | 55.5 | 52.3 |
| 1983–84 | 52.8 | 48.1 |
| 1984–85 | 56.8 | 53.1 |
| 1985–86[5] | 65.0 | 62.6 |
| 1986–87 | 63.5 | 62.2 |
| 1987–88 | 65.0 | 62.5 |
| 1988–89[6] | 47.3 | 41.3 |
| 1989–90 | 47.3 | 40.2 |
| 1990–91 | 49.2 | 42.0 |
| 1991–92[7] | 46.4 | 38.3 |

[1] District 4 opened first alternative "choice" middle school.
[2] City switched from Metropolitan Achievement Test to Stanford Achievement Test. Teachers and principals call the new test "easier."
[3] City switched from Stanford Achievement Test to California Achievement Test.
[4] District 4 declared districtwide "choice" policy for all middle schools.
[5] City changed from California Achievement Test to Degrees of Reading Power.
[6] Citywide reading test renormed to higher national standard.
[7] 1991–92 results are preliminary.
SOURCE: Information from the New York City Board of Education compiled by The Carnegie Foundation for the Advancement of Teaching.

talking about family problems, physical and sexual abuse. We're talking about 13-year-old girls with 25-year-old boyfriends. Runaways. Kids with alcohol- or drug-abusing parents. It's not just academics. These are deep-seated problems."

Another cautionary note from East Harlem concerns the way program directors are battling one another for the "better" students—

"better" defined not necessarily by test scores or academic achievement but by signs of effort and motivation. While each school insists it is willing to take its share of "bad apples," as one administrator put it, there is a growing sense that a few well-publicized schools are getting more than their share of capable students, while others get many deeply troubled ones. One program director put it ruefully: "After Manhattan East, Harbor School, and Isaac Newton School, it's kind of a Reagan trickle-down theory."

To their lasting credit, the leaders of District 4 continue to confront these issues of equity and excellence. One of the clearest accomplishments directly attributable to school choice is District 4's exemplary record of scrapping problem schools that fail year after year to attract students. This past winter, John Falco, the current Director of Alternative Schools, held a series of frank, sometimes heated meetings with program directors to discuss how to mediate the competition for motivated students. As a result, the district has quietly modified its admissions procedures to widen the mix of students in each program and give the district board a somewhat expanded role as referee.

Today, nearly twenty years after the first alternative schools opened, East Harlem offers a glimpse—one of the very few in America—of a maturing "choice" system in a community with severe social and economic problems. Do the changes and innovative spirit survive after the pioneering leaders have left and the start-up money has dried up? Does the "Hawthorne effect" of choice—the positive changes that result purely from the initial burst of excitement that something daring is being done—carry over in later years?

In East Harlem, the verdict seems to be this: Some, though by no means all, of choice's initial benefits have survived the test of time. For a combination of reasons, student achievement as measured by standardized tests rose considerably in the early years of choice, but has fallen off more recently. And while money played a big part in choice's early success, lack of money is now playing an equally critical part in eroding some of those gains.

"There has been an enormous amount of mythmaking about choice in District 4," said Alvarado recently. "Choice is just one arrow in the strategic quiver. District 4 did not succeed just because of choice. We got loads of money to deal with innovation. Bold leadership was an extraordinary factor. At the same time, District 4 employed some very traditional principals, some of whom had the biggest test score gains. You can't tell me what an improvement is due to."

If there's a single lesson from East Harlem, then, it's that choice is anything but a quick, easy path to school betterment. District 4's pioneering choice system has surely contributed to progress. By some measures, student performance has improved. Parents do feel more empowered, and teachers feel they have an opportunity to be far more creative. Overall, we were impressed by the vitality of the district. Still, with all the progress, choice cannot be cited as a silver bullet of reform.

Montclair, Cambridge, and East Harlem have not solved all their problems. They have, however, proven that choice in a single district can stimulate creative planning and promote widespread satisfaction. Because of choice there is a strong desire in these districts to continue innovating, to offer more and better options, and above all, to distribute opportunities fairly to all children. Choice has succeeded as well as it has in these places primarily because communities have worked together to shape a strategy for reform.

The experiences of these "stars of choice" can only guide, not firmly answer, whether other districts should follow their example. That decision properly belongs to each community—not the statehouse or the White House.

# CHAPTER 4

## Statewide Choice: Winners and Losers

I N 1986, THE NATIONAL GOVERNORS' ASSOCIATION added its prestigious voice to those calling for school choice. Here's how the governors framed the challenge: "Schools that compete for students, teachers, and dollars will, by virtue of their environment, make those changes that allow them to succeed."[1] With this gubernatorial blessing, the "choice" movement soon swept entire states. In 1987, Minnesota became the first in the nation to grant students broad rights to attend virtually any school in the state for any reason. Twelve others have followed, permitting students far greater freedom to choose schools outside their resident districts.[2]

Advocates believe that statewide choice will extend new educational opportunities to students, add the tonic of marketplace competition, and stimulate widespread school improvement. "There need to be some incentives to improve. I think all school systems will improve because of the competition," says William Bulger, president of the Massachusetts State Senate. He, together with Governor William Weld, engineered that state's year-old "choice" system, which overnight transformed the financial fortunes of school districts—for better *and* worse.

Besides Minnesota, states with comprehensive choice programs now include Arkansas, Idaho, Iowa, Massachusetts, Nebraska, and Utah. More restricted arrangements can be found in Alabama, Arizona, California, Colorado, Oregon, and Washington. Also actively considering choice are Alaska, North Dakota, and Virginia. And beginning in the 1993–94 school year, every school district in Michigan with more than one school at a grade level must develop and implement a "schools of choice" plan or risk losing state funding. Ohio, which currently permits transfers between bordering districts, also requires that all districts develop a "choice" policy by 1993.

47

In November 1992, Colorado voters turned down a citizen initiative that would have given vouchers worth up to $2,500 to parents who send their children to private or parochial schools, or who educate their youngsters at home.

In California, a similar voucher initiative was removed from the November 1992 ballot by the state supreme court due to the lack of validated signatures. It is expected that backers will try again in June 1994. The California initiative, which has the support of business, would grant all students in the state requesting it a "scholarship" equal to at least 50 percent of local and state per-student costs, usable at any public or private school. This state already has a modified "choice" plan that allows parents to switch their children to public schools in the districts where they work. Some fifteen to twenty thousand have done so.

In all states with "choice" programs, parent participation is voluntary. Still, there are practical restrictions. In fast-growing Washington, for example, popular districts have not been able to take all of the applicants. In 1991, 48 percent more requests for transfers were denied than in the previous year because of limited space.[3] Meanwhile, in Minnesota, few white students have been allowed to transfer from Minneapolis schools because of the city's desegregation plan. However, both Minneapolis and St. Paul do operate extensive intradistrict magnet programs. In Alabama, many of the largest school systems are effectively barred from interdistrict choice because of desegregation court orders. Likewise, mandates for racial balance have slowed the growth of Arkansas' "choice" plan, and in Iowa, interdistrict transfers are restricted by desegregation plans in a dozen districts.

Most statewide "choice" systems are still in their infancy, leaving many questions unanswered about their potential. What is clearest is that, thus far, few students have taken advantage of their new-found right to switch: In Arkansas, 1,667 students—about four-tenths of one percent of the state's public school population—attend schools outside their districts under the 1989 choice plan. Nearly ten thousand Washington students, about 1.2 percent of the state's pupils, participate in interdistrict "choice" programs under the 1990 "Learning by Choice" law. Some five thousand Colorado students are attending schools outside their district under a 1990 choice law—less than .9 percent of the state's enrollment. Idaho adopted a statewide open enrollment law in 1990 and some 2,580 students—or 1.2 percent—participated during the 1991–92 school year. More than 5,000 Iowa students, about 1 percent of the state's total, currently participate in a statewide plan adopted in 1989. Massachusetts' year-old open enrollment program attracted 1,100 students in 1991–92—about .1 percent of that state's students. Nebraska's 1989 program involves 3,300 students—1.2 percent of total enrollment. In Minnesota, some thirteen thousand students attended public schools outside their district in 1991–92 under open enroll-ment—about 1.8 percent of the student body.[4]

Why have so few students crossed district lines? There are, as we said, constraints as a result of desegregation plans and lack of available space. Beyond that, one obvious explanation is that most parents and students are satisfied with their neighborhood schools, or at least not dissatisfied enough to switch. Another reason may well be that choice has failed to deliver on its promise to create more diverse educational options. In other words, ''choice'' exists but there are few distinctive choices. The public school in the next town doesn't offer anything re-markably different from the one just around the corner.

Another likely explanation is that virtually no state provides enough transportation assistance to make choice meaningful. A few, like Iowa, Minnesota, Nebraska, Washington, and Ohio, offer at least some help. By and large, however, most states leave the transportation up to par-ents and local school districts. Concerns about transportation costs, in-deed, led Michigan's legislature to postpone a statewide plan; the extra state transportation aid was estimated at $20 million.

Then, too, information for parents is a hit-or-miss proposition. Minnesota is an exception. This state disseminates an array of pam-phlets and guides. Idaho requires each school to publish an annual ''re-port card.'' In most states, however, reliable information about school options is scarce. Further, no state has effectively addressed the need to monitor the accuracy of promotional materials published by districts seeking to attract students.

Statewide programs have undeniably helped some parents and stu-dents find new, more satisfying opportunities. Some participants are opting for the intimacy of a smaller school. Others are switching to larger schools offering more stimulation and curricular variety. Still others simply want to be with friends, or attend schools with the better gym or hockey club. Many parents are transferring their children to schools nearer their jobs, or closer to day care.

In Iowa the open enrollment application asks parents to indicate the most important reason for leaving their neighborhood schools. In 1990–91, barely one-third, or 32 percent, cited "educational benefits," 26 percent cited "family convenience," 16 percent said "proximity to job or home," and 10 percent said "school philosophy or values" were paramount.[5]

A 1989 survey of Arizona students who switched schools found that one-third did so for academic reasons, while the remainder cited proximity to home, day care, or work; specialized or special education programs; sports and athletics; and other reasons.[6] A survey of Minnesota parents whose children transferred under open enrollment in 1989–90 found that 55 percent cited "learning climate" as a motive. Many, however, gave reasons related to convenience, such as geographic proximity, day care considerations, or parents working in another district.[7]

Arkansas state officials say that they can't draw clear conclusions on this issue because too few students have switched schools. But in Cushman, Arkansas, for example, twenty students have transferred under school choice from its larger neighbor, Batesville, and another twenty-five are expected to do so this year. Cushman's superintendent Gary Anderson attributes the transfers more to his district's smaller size than to its relative quality: "This has nothing to do with Batesville being bad," he said. "A lot of it also has to do with convenience. My own kids go to Batesville schools. But Batesville operates classes with thirty kids. Ours are roughly half that, so there's more individual attention. And because we're a smaller district, there are more extracurricular opportunities here." At $2,500 per student in state aid, choice has meant a $100,000-plus windfall for Cushman.

For high school senior Becky Haehnel, open enrollment in Minnesota meant she could switch from her small school in tiny Motley to a larger one in Staples ten miles away to take part in the Future Farmers of America program. Tenth-grader Lara Emstad, of Wells, Minnesota, is pleased with her chosen high school in Alden eight miles away because the smaller school expanded her opportunities to participate in interscholastic sports. Fourteen-year-old Shirley Allioth was able to escape overcrowded Brockton, Massachusetts, schools and attend nearby suburban Avon Middle-High School, where class sizes average less than twenty. "I'm into sports, and I couldn't get into it as easily in Brockton," she said. "Here I'm playing volleyball, basketball, and I'll be in softball this spring."

Beyond such anecdotes, harsher realities are encountered. The free market system is, we discovered, creating an entirely new landscape of educational winners and losers, with serious, often unforeseen consequences for struggling school districts—and for children. Little-known places like Exira, Iowa; Cushman, Arkansas; Motley, Montgomery-Lonsdale, and New Prague, Minnesota; and Brockton and Avon, Massachusetts, have been dramatically changed by the sudden gain or loss of students or dollars—often for reasons having less to do with educational quality than with the accidents of location, size, or relative wealth.

In almost every statewide plan, districts that lose students lose funding, too. State funding follows students in Arkansas, Colorado, Minnesota, Idaho, Ohio, Nebraska, Washington, and Utah. State money, plus a portion of *local* funds, follows students in Iowa, California, and Utah. This feature, more than anything else, makes statewide choice more complicated and questionable than districtwide choice, which involves no such cross-district transfers of students and aid dollars.

Minnesota, the heartland of statewide choice, offers a wide variety of options. Along with open enrollment, there's a "postsecondary option" program allowing high school juniors and seniors to take college courses. The state also has "second-chance" and alternative programs for dropouts or high-risk students who don't succeed in traditional schools. In 1991, the Minnesota legislature inaugurated the nation's first "charter" schools program, which grants teachers and others the opportunity to create their own schools. These charter schools will be state funded but largely free of government control. They have three years to live up to achievement goals or risk losing their charters.

What's the evidence that Minnesota's choice plan is working? In addition to a low participation rate—less than 2 percent of all students—there are few signs that choice has sparked educational renewal. State education officials claim that choice has spurred growth in the advanced placement programs "several times over."[8] In fact, the number of schools offering such courses has risen only slightly since the advent of choice—from 125 in 1989 to 147 in 1992, out of 497 high schools.[9] Even more revealing, only 9 percent of the districts have made curricular changes as a result of open enrollment. The biggest change, we learned—as cited by superintendents—was an increase in average class size, either because new students were entering a district or because student departures from a district forced program or teacher cuts.[10]

A survey asking Minnesota school administrators to weigh the impact of choice found that 89 percent said it had no effect on diversifying teaching styles, and 80 percent said it had done nothing to spur instructional innovation.[11]

Undeniably, some Minnesota districts have been hurt by choice. Further, 22 percent of the state's superintendents have indicated that choice would have a "mostly negative" impact on their district's finances.[12] In 1991, Motley, a northern Minnesota farm town of about 450, lost 239 pupils to neighboring Staples, a ten-minute drive away. It also lost $838,000 in state aid. The high school in Staples boasts more facilities and course offerings than its small-town neighbor: computer labs, a music library, and a gym festooned with more than one hundred state and regional championship flags. It's hard to imagine how Motley can compete successfully with Staples. However, one student who didn't make the switch told us: "There are more class offerings in Staples, but you get a lot more help here."

The Montgomery-Lonsdale district, located some thirty-five miles south of the Twin Cities, has lost some sixty students to nearby New Prague, according to superintendent Harvey Kane. He says that "90-plus percent" of the reasons parents give for switching schools have nothing to do with the quality of programs, but with the availability of day care and the fact that New Prague is conveniently located on their daily commute to the Twin Cities. The result: Montgomery-Lonsdale is $200,000 poorer because of statewide choice. "We find ourselves in a financial bind, and frankly there's not a damned thing we can do about it," Kane said.

Lewis Finch, former superintendent of the 33,000-student Anoka-Hennepin School District in Coon Rapids, Minnesota, wrote that "virtually all" of the several hundred transfer requests handled by his office "were based on convenience and location, rather than on the quality of education in a given school."[13]

The evidence is not wholly one-sided. Tiny Minnesota districts like Randall, Miltona, Delavan, Cyrus, and Morris, in order to compete, have established some of the nation's first rural magnet schools specializing in math, science, and technology. S. G. Knight Elementary School in Randall became a science magnet four years ago. It now boasts a thirty-terminal computer lab and a hands-on environmental science lab that engages students from kindergarten on. About sixty students from other communities take bus rides of up to an hour and ten minutes to attend this farm-town school. One parent, whose son travels twelve miles each day to Randall from neighboring Swanville, explained her switch: "I don't want to sound like a bragging parent, but my son was talented in math. I wanted more for him."

But choice was not the only factor. S. G. Knight's transformation from a traditional elementary school to a well-equipped science magnet was helped along by exemplary leadership, and generous outside funding. The district received a $15,000 federal grant and another $17,000 from the University of Minnesota's Center for School Change. Such grants enabled Knight teachers to have special science training that led to the school's outdoor environmental science curriculum. Just as crucial was the effective leadership of district superintendent Kerry Jacobson and principal Dan Bakke.

Alden, Minnesota, another small-town "choice" winner, is located about ten miles north of the Iowa border. This little district has attracted 56 of its 406 students from neighboring districts including Albert Lea, Freeborn, Richland, and Wells. Among Alden's attractions: creative and caring school leaders, solid community backing for education, special programs for high-schoolers with reading problems, a deep commitment to values education in the elementary grades, and restructured class periods allowing students time for one-on-one instruction with any teacher. Elementary principal Guy Spence has ably led the way.

Suburban South St. Paul also has profited from choice. This district, which aggressively markets itself with ads and brochures, has gained one hundred students from nearby districts and parochial schools. Administrators credit overall academic quality, and especially an "International Baccalaureate" program that features language and liberal arts study. But our examination of its open enrollment applications revealed that, beyond academics, what sold many parents and students on South St. Paul were day care availability, convenience, or friends at the school.

Indeed, many parents base their school choice decisions on factors that have nothing to do with the quality of education. Occasionally they even use their new-found freedom to make unreasonable demands. One administrator told us about a straight-A student and star athlete in a small northern school district who wanted to play interscholastic hockey. His home district had no hockey team, but a town nearby did. The student and his parents demanded that the school assume the $1,000 cost of allowing him to play in the neighboring program. After lengthy meetings, the school board refused. The student transferred out of the district, taking about $4,000 in state aid with him. In this case, the board resisted an unreasonable demand. But if very many families had made this request, it's not hard to imagine that a small district might have yielded.

Another Minnesota superintendent cited a case in which a parent used the threat of open enrollment to pressure his district to resolve a liability suit: "A kid was horsing around on the playground and broke his collarbone. The parent says, 'If you don't pay for the medical bills, I will go to the board and publicly criticize you for improper supervision, and I will send my three kids out of your district.' The medical bill was less than $700. The state aid for the three kids was $12,500. I told the parents, 'The school district can't pay for legal reasons, but I'll give the case to our insurance company for possible resolution.' If the insurance doesn't pay, we'll lose those kids."

The central issue here is not whether most parents make "good" or "bad" choices for their children. The more urgent question is whether choice will promote school improvement. From what we've observed, there is no clear evidence that choice in Minnesota has been a transforming influence for most schools.

In the Commonwealth of Massachusetts a statewide choice plan has had a remarkable impact, but not the kind its architects intended. Here's the background. Early in the morning of June 14, 1991, a marathon legislative session ended with the Massachusetts Senate approving its version of the state's fiscal 1992 budget. Buried in that document was an amendment, nondescriptly titled Section 304, that authorized school choice throughout the state.

Participation in the Massachusetts plan is "voluntary" in the sense that a district can choose not to accept outside students. However, no district can deny students the freedom to leave. In the first year, only 32 of the state's 361 districts opted into choice. Among the hold-outs have been wealthy suburbs like Brookline, which fear that head-to-head competition for students and dollars might poison relations with neighboring Boston. Still, Peter R. Finn, director of the State Superintendents Association, whose executive committee unanimously opposed the current plan, believes that the threat of lost state aid will cause a "domino effect" that will eventually force most districts to participate. Districts that don't would simply lose students, with no possibility of gaining any.

In the year since it took effect, the Massachusetts plan has been hailed by some as opening doors of opportunity long denied to less well-off students. One parent, Susan Andersen, transferred her child last year from Mount Everett High School to Monument High School in the Berkshire Mountains. She wrote: "I'm impressed by the student-centered atmosphere, the abundance of course offerings at different levels, the high quality of guidance services, the athletic department and the cordial, yet professional decorum of all of the administrators, support staff and teachers I have met."[14]

Many others, including some of choice's staunchest allies, have called the program "destructive" and "irresponsible."[15] The Massachusetts plan as originally constructed virtually assured that financially distressed districts would grow weaker. "That's the stupidity of our choice plan," said William Hosmer, superintendent of the Hopkinton school system. His district lost fifty-six of its fifteen hundred students to its larger neighbor, Holliston, and was forced to drop an elementary librarian and cut back on remedial reading and math programs.

Why did choice prove so unfortunate in Massachusetts?

For one thing it's hard to imagine a state more poorly suited for choice. The Bay State is among the nation's more inequitable in terms of school funding. In 1990, the poorest districts spent about $2,800 per pupil, the wealthiest more than $8,600. Further, school districts in Massachusetts are unusually dependent on their local tax base. Proposition 2½, passed by state voters a decade ago, sharply limits future property tax increases. Today, the state share of public school funding is just 36.9 percent, which puts Massachusetts forty-third out of fifty.

Finally, the state has been severely hit by the recession. It's ironic that at the very moment "choice" districts were being asked to compete for students and state aid, many were churning out press releases detailing teacher layoffs, textbook and supply cutbacks, larger classes, and crumbling school buildings—hardly the ideal sales pitch for attracting students. "The commonwealth is stacking the odds before the game begins," said Gregory Ciardi, superintendent of schools in Maynard, a suburb northwest of Boston which lost 52 of its 1,250 students and $312,000 in aid to its wealthier neighbor, Acton.[16]

During the first year of operation, the Massachusetts plan was the most punitive in the nation. It made sending districts responsible for the full per-pupil cost of educating each student it lost to another district, even when that district's per student expenditures were far higher. For example, Gloucester, a relatively poor district north of Boston, spent less than $4,500 per pupil. Yet each time one of its students switched to its wealthier neighbor, Manchester-by-the-Sea, Gloucester lost state funding equal to the full $7,677 that Manchester spent per pupil. According to superintendent William Leary, Gloucester lost 77 of its thirty-seven hundred pupils to Manchester in 1991–92, translating to a loss of $410,000 in state aid alone. "It doesn't take the loss of many students before you have lost serious, serious money," said William

Crowley, who recently retired as executive assistant state superintendent.

The Massachusetts law also phased out existing arrangements in which students willing and wealthy enough to pay tuition could attend neighboring districts. Forty-eight of the seventy-seven students who "open-enrolled" from Gloucester to Manchester during the 1991–92 school year had already been attending Manchester schools, with parents paying Manchester $3,500 in tuition. Under the new school choice arrangement, the tuition bill, once paid by parents, abruptly shifted to the Gloucester school district, which thus lost state aid for students who were already attending Manchester schools before choice started. And Manchester charged Gloucester not the $3,500 that parents once paid, but $6,500![17]

The impact of all this can best be illustrated by looking at the financially distressed city of Brockton and its tiny neighbor, Avon. There is convenient public transportation between the two towns. Every twenty minutes a Brockton Area Transportation bus drops Brockton kids off right in front of Avon Middle-High School, and a monthly ticket costs just eighteen dollars. Under choice, students could easily cross district lines, and many did.

Avon desperately needed students. Many classes had fewer than ten children. The entire senior class had only twenty-one pupils. That explained why Avon's per-student spending was among the state's highest: $10,239 at the high school level. For three years before the advent of choice, Avon had aggressively advertised for tuition-paying students from other districts, attracting thirty-one in 1989 and fifty-one in 1991. Each paid $1,800 to attend. But the new law called for phasing out this program, which posed a further threat to Avon. "We had powerful motives to participate in choice," said superintendent Lincoln Lynch. He agreed that the Massachusetts plan has created "havoc and destruction," especially for cities like Brockton. But the bottom line for Avon was that choice made good business sense. "We had no choice but to take choice," said Lynch.

Brockton, meanwhile, is nearly broke and has been placed under the supervision of a state financial control board. Efforts to attract industry and boost its tax base have not been successful. Avon, by contrast, draws half of its school revenues from tax receipts from a local industrial park, allowing it to impose a lighter tax burden on homeowners.

With the coming of choice, Avon immediately reaped a bonanza of students and more dollars. In the first year of the program, the district attracted 135 students from nearby Brockton. According to Avon Middle-High School principal Henry Jay Levine, enrollment in grades five through twelve rose from 333 in 1990, to 414 in 1991. Choice also brought the district a $900,000 windfall—enough, said Levine, to hire a new guidance counselor, upgrade technology, buy new texts, and even pay for a new roof for his school.

Students making the switch seemed pleased with their decision. They liked the intimate environment and smaller classes. Harold "Chip" Heaton, a senior from Brockton who attended Avon High as a "choice" student, says the thirty-five-minute bus ride each day "has changed my life around completely. In the other school it was easy to slide. I got away with murder. I was getting truant and into other things. Here, I get a lot of individual help."

The picture is far grimmer for the 14,500 students left behind in Brockton. Choice simply worsened an already difficult situation, says superintendent Manthala George. Cuts in state aid—forced by the new choice law—meant that Brockton opened the 1991 school year with its $48 million budget reduced by nearly $6 million. Choice brought an added loss of $933,000 in state aid in 1992. "The real laugh," George said, "is that in fiscal 1989, our budget was $49.5 million. In 1990, it was $48.1 million. In 1991, it was $48.3 million. This year, it's $42.9 million. So in 1992 we lose 250 positions, of whom two hundred are teachers, or 24 percent of our locally funded teaching staff."

Because of budget cuts and layoffs, some Brockton classes swelled to forty or more. Elementary choral and instrumental music programs were eliminated, and counseling and library services were cut back. Junior high foreign-language, athletic, and intramural programs were dropped. At Brockton High, the reading department was cut, courses in virtually all disciplines were reduced, and the supply budget was slashed by 44 percent. Twenty-two administrative positions were eliminated.

In the year since choice began, the Massachusetts legislature has taken steps to ease the adverse impact on poor districts. As an emergency measure, it appropriated $2.7 million in one-time aid. Brockton received enough to hire back 40 percent of its laid-off teachers and reduce some class sizes. The legislature also capped the amount of money a receiving district can get at $5,000. Districts losing pupils are reimbursed 75 percent of their losses by the state. The state also, for the first time, guaranteed transferring students the right to remain in their chosen district until graduation. Finally, the revised plan mandated that a parent information system be established by the state secretary of education. Such changes represent a welcome softening of some of the harsher features of the Massachusetts plan.

Massachusetts lawmakers failed, however, to approve a transportation subsidy, which means that the plan works better for some students than others. If the state of Massachusetts had agreed to reimburse the transportation costs incurred by all students who took part in choice last year (at the state employee reimbursement rate of 22 cents per mile), that would have added more than $1,500 to the cost of educating each transferring pupil. With 1,100 students participating, transportation costs would have been about $1.7 million, assuming two car trips per day of ten miles each.[18]

Even with the changes, districts like Brockton see little reason to cheer. Officials in that district say they still could lose about $350,000 to $400,000 in the 1992–93 school year. These losses, coupled with other financial problems, may mean more teacher layoffs and larger classes. District officials believe Avon may try to make up for the smaller state reimbursement by admitting still more Brockton students.

In Gloucester, superintendent William Leary says that choice will probably cost his district more than $150,000 in lost aid, with 120 students expected to leave in 1992–93.

"Telling school districts to improve or lose money is simply a cynical and absurd argument," Leary told us.

What are we to conclude from all of this?

From what we have observed, academic quality is often not the primary reason for participating in statewide "choice" programs. It therefore seems unlikely that choice alone will, through competition, lift the quality of schools. Indeed, questions about the educational effectiveness of choice, as well as the costs, have led twenty-one state legislatures to reject such plans in the last five years, according to Carnegie's Survey of Chief State School Officers. Some advocates of choice have expressed disappointment about achievements to date. Prof. Mary Ann Raywid, of Hofstra University, for example, makes this telling point: "Open enrollment arrangements, which now exist in a number of states, have not led to the diversification among schools that market loyalists predicted and which their case requires."[19] Roger Hudson, director of Nebraska's three-year-old Enrollment Options Program, puts it even more clearly: "School improvement? That's a pipe dream. I believe in the free market system. But until you see real data, that's all fun and games."

Above all, we are convinced that no statewide choice program should be established until some essential requirements have been met. First and foremost, districts participating in statewide choice must compete on an even playing field. Common sense argues that a district spending $3,000 to $4,000 per pupil should not be asked to compete with one spending two or three times as much. And yet the reality is that in thirty-nine states, the richest districts spend at least twice as much per pupil as the poorest. In eight—California, Illinois, Montana, New York, North Dakota, Texas, Utah, and Washington—the richest district spends more than four times as much.[20] In thirteen states, choice has been imposed on districts with great spending discrepancies.

It was clear from our study that few if any students transferred from a rich district to a poor one. If fair competition is to occur, all states with "choice" programs must first resolve the financial disparities that exist from district to district. Until this goal is realized, choice will widen the gap between the privileged and the disadvantaged and make a mockery of the goal of equality and opportunity for all.

Further, every statewide "choice" program requires a parent information system, one that makes program details available to all parents and spells out how school selections should be made. We found no state where this essential obligation has been satisfactorily fulfilled. Indeed, in most states where choice has been introduced, the laws are silent on

60

consumer information about schools. Parents are generally in the dark, not only about the quality of schools nearby, but even about how the system of choosing works.

Next, every state adopting a school ''choice'' plan must provide for student transportation. It's simply irresponsible to introduce choice and fail to make arrangements for those who need to be transported to and from school. Choice usually means traveling to a more distant school. If parents are required to transport their children, this may be prohibitively inconvenient and discriminate against the poorest families. If, on the other hand, schools accept the responsibility, transportation costs surely will increase.

According to one estimate, school districts now spend, on average, about $233 per pupil each year on transportation, or about 4.4 percent of total per-student expenditures. Overall, transportation costs total about $9.5 billion nationwide. If choice ever caught on as a truly national reform—to the point where, say, even 10 percent of the nation's 42 million students attended public schools outside their district—billions of dollars would be added to the nation's school bus tab. Still, for states with ''choice'' plans, it is a price that, for the sake of equity, must be paid.

Finally, we are troubled that most statewide plans have been so swiftly and arbitrarily imposed. While public referendum may not be an essential precondition, it does not seem unreasonable to suggest that parents should be advised of the proposed change and asked for their opinions. Local school boards, administrators, and teachers should also be given time before the new plans are enacted to consider the ramifications of choice and to express their views.

In summary, the early history of existing plans leaves us doubtful about the prospects for achieving fair, effective statewide choice. Surely prospects for success as well as equity are dramatically diminished when programs are not undergirded by fair funding, effective parent-information programs, and the assurance that all students will be transported to the schools of choice.

Some supporters of choice, too, address the issue of preconditions. Boston University professor Charles L. Glenn, for example, a leading authority and advocate of choice, argues that a sound system should include "procedures to assure equal access, effective outreach and individual counseling, and measures to assure that there are real educational choices available." He emphasizes that "an effective school choice program does not involve only the most motivated and sophisticated parents, nor does it accept a situation in which a few schools—and communities—are perceived as highly desirable while others retain only those pupils who do not or cannot escape."[21]

By any standard of fairness, then, statewide programs demand a level playing field. At minimum, this means adequate transportation for all students; accessible, reliable information for parents and students about the plan itself and about the quality of schools and their programs; and serious attention to reducing the huge disparities between rich and poor districts. By these yardsticks, we conclude that responsible and effective statewide school choice does not exist in America today.

# CHAPTER 5

## *Private-School Choice: Milwaukee*

THE NATION'S MOST ENTHUSIASTIC ADVOCATES of choice insist that private schools should be among the options available to all parents. President Bush speaks firmly about the need to extend choice to "all schools that serve the public and are accountable to public authority, regardless of who runs them." Proponents say that such a strategy, often called a "voucher plan," would open a rich array of educational options to all students and give to less affluent families opportunities for learning that now are available mainly to the privileged. Further, involving nonpublic schools in choice programs would, says U.S. Secretary of Education Lamar Alexander, "unleash marketplace forces that would help make all schools better."[1]

It's unclear just where Americans stand on vouchers. As is so often the case, it seems to depend on how the proposition is worded and who is asked. In a 1991 Gallup poll of the American public about half the respondents said they favored the idea of school vouchers, 39 percent were opposed, while 11 percent were uncertain. Even higher percentages of minorities (57 percent), nonpublic school parents (66 percent), and inner-city dwellers (57 percent) favored the voucher concept.[2] In a similar poll conducted in 1992, 70 percent of the respondents said they would support a government voucher plan that would enable parents to send their children to any school—public, private, or parochial.[3] As we discussed in chapter two, in our own national poll of *parents*, we asked if families should be given a voucher to enroll children in private schools at public expense, and only about one-third supported the idea.

Survey results may vary. What is indisputable, however, is that in less than five years, the drive to include nonpublic schools in "choice" plans has moved from the edge of the school reform debate toward center stage. Private-school choice proposals have surfaced in legislatures in at least thirteen states, according to Carnegie's Survey of Chief State School Officers. None has been approved either by the legislatures or popular referendum.

In the most significant electoral test thus far, Oregon voters rejected, by a wide margin, a voucher initiative in 1990, and Colorado citizens likewise voted against a voucher measure in 1992. Pro-voucher groups in California failed to get the signatures needed to put a similar measure before voters, but supporters are expected to try again. And last June, groups of poor parents in Los Angeles and Chicago sued their respective school districts, demanding the right to send their children to private schools at public expense.[4]

Meanwhile, some business leaders have come forward to promote the idea. In Indianapolis, the Golden Rule Insurance Co. created an "Educational Choice Charitable Trust," which promises to pay up to $800 to help a family send an elementary school child to a nonpublic school. "We intend this as a direct challenge to the Indianapolis Public Schools: improve or lose students," said J. Patrick Rooney, chairman of the company. In San Antonio, a group of business and foundation leaders set up a $1.5 million voucher fund to send up to 750 children to nonpublic schools. More than thirteen hundred applications were received within two weeks. And in Milwaukee, Wisconsin, a private group called Partners Advancing Values in Education began a voucher plan financed by the Lynde and Harry Bradley Foundation.

To date, however, Milwaukee is the only place in the country with a *publicly* financed private-school choice plan. The two-year-old Milwaukee experiment has become, according to Secretary Alexander, "America's pioneer in giving middle- and low-income parents consumer power—dollars to use at the schools of their choice. This consumer power is the muscle that parents need to create the best schools in the world for their children. This is exactly the kind of revolution that President Bush believes is necessary to change our schools."[5]

Milwaukee was a city ripe for change. Sixty percent of its children live below the poverty line, and 28 percent of minority families are unemployed. The teen pregnancy rate is double the national average; twenty-five hundred children are homeless. The student turnover rate is as high as 70 percent in some schools, and the dropout rate is 40 percent. Some 6,300 children are bused to suburbs each day under the state-sponsored "Chapter 220" integration plan, while another 19,000 elementary school children are bused outside their neighborhoods because their own schools are so overcrowded.

There are bright spots in this grim picture. For years, the district has operated an extensive magnet-school program. Recently Brown Academy was opened, offering extended day programs for elementary school youngsters. There are Montessori schools, gifted and talented magnets, and a number of well-regarded neighborhood public schools such as Lee Avenue School, Garfield School, Lloyd Street School, and Rufus King High School, among others.

Even with these innovative efforts, though, the city's schools overall have remained deeply troubled. During the 1980s, two state commissions documented Milwaukee's problems and laid out solutions. A 1988 report even proposed a "Marshall Plan" for the city's schools. But few of these reform proposals were ever implemented, according to Tom Fonfara, a senior policy analyst in Wisconsin governor Tommy Thompson's office. State funding for Milwaukee's 97,000-pupil school district nearly tripled during the 1980s—from $129 million in 1980–81 to $310 million in 1991–92—yet even this was insufficient to address the district's severe problems.

It was against this backdrop that in 1987 a group of black legislators and community leaders, including state representative Annette "Polly" Williams, began to promote the idea of an all-black school district in Milwaukee. For years, Williams and others were angered not only by chronic school problems but also by the fact that black children were taking long bus rides in search of quality education. "Polly never liked Section 220, and she's right about this," said Herbert J. Grover, state school superintendent and a leading critic of Milwaukee's "choice" plan. "How would you like your third grader bused miles every day?"

Unable to build support for a separate black district, Williams teamed with Governor Thompson to promote private-school choice. She had sent her own children to the private Urban Day School. Private-school choice, she believed, would put quality education within the reach of poor families. Thompson, for his part, was a long-time advocate of choice and had campaigned unsuccessfully for a statewide plan that would include parochial schools. The governor then settled for the more limited Milwaukee program. Also supportive was Milwaukee mayor John O. Norquist, who said that the urban school system should be "scrapped" and replaced with "a choice or voucher system."

The Wisconsin legislature authorized the Milwaukee plan, which was upheld by a 4 to 3 vote by the Wisconsin Supreme Court in March 1992. In a concurring opinion, Justice Louis J. Ceci wrote: "The Wisconsin legislature has attempted to throw a life preserver to those Milwaukee children caught in the cruel riptide of a school system floundering upon the shoals of poverty, status quo thinking, and despair."

Under the Milwaukee plan, public school students may attend private, nonsectarian schools in the city. Each participating school receives approximately $2,600 per student—the average amount paid by the state to the public schools. Receiving schools may provide busing, for which they are reimbursed by the state, or parents may provide transportation themselves. Those parents who do so are reimbursed at the end of the school year.

There are restrictions, however. The program is geared to serve disadvantaged families—those with incomes below 1.75 times the poverty level (about $22,000 for a family of three). Also, participation is limited to just 1 percent of the city's public school population—or just under one thousand students. Participating students are randomly selected, although some sibling preference is permitted. During the first year, 341 students, almost all of whom were nonwhites, transferred to private schools. The number increased to 562 in 1991, and rose again the following year to 632.

Milwaukee has eighteen nonsectarian private schools. As of 1991, only six elected to participate. Four private elementary and middle schools enrolled about 90 percent of the children: Bruce-Guadalupe Bilingual Community School, Harambee Community School, Urban Day School, and Woodlands School. The other two participating schools were Lakeshore Montessori School and an alternative high school called SER-Jobs for Progress. In 1992, five more schools joined the program. The rest have stayed out, according to University of Wisconsin Professor John F. Witte, either because the $2,600 voucher doesn't cover costs, or because of a concern that the program, in time, might entangle them in a web of regulations.

As it turns out, the Milwaukee plan was devised to provide the least possible state oversight of private schools. After all, the reasoning went, if the choice program overregulated private schools, they soon would resemble the bureaucracy-laden public schools. Further, private schools made it clear they would resist any plan with onerous regulatory strings. As a result, requirements in the Milwaukee plan are hardly burdensome. Participating schools must meet only *one* of the following four standards: First, at least 70 percent of "choice" students at the school must advance one grade level each year; second, average attendance must reach at least 90 percent; third, at least 80 percent of all participating students must demonstrate "significant" academic progress; *or*, fourth, at least 70 percent of the families of "choice" pupils must meet the parental involvement criteria set by the private school.

It's revealing that in the first year, three out of the six private schools met their requirement by simply submitting their attendance records. Two schools used the parental involvement criteria. Only one—SER-Jobs for Progress—submitted evidence of its students' academic progress. According to Julie Underwood, co-director of the University of Wisconsin's Center for Educational Policy, the state has thus allowed participating private schools to be "self-declared effective without adequate accountability."

The dangers of this regulatory vacuum soon became apparent in the case of Juanita Virgil Academy. In the first year of the program, this school enrolled sixty-three "choice" students but shut down in the middle of the year amid charges of mismanagement, lack of books and supplies, overcrowding, and poor discipline. The Juanita Virgil fiasco confronted Milwaukee with the stark reality that when marketplace ideas fail, children suffer.

Professor Witte, a self-described advocate of choice, writes in his "First Year Report" on the Milwaukee plan: "There are those who would argue that the failure of [Juanita Virgil] is to be expected in a market system of education. Whether one believes that expectation outweighs the fact that approximately 150 children essentially lost a year's education is a value issue that we cannot resolve. Whatever one's values are, the price was high for those families involved.'' Witte has urged the Wisconsin legislature to tighten the Milwaukee plan. The state, he insists, should require participating schools to submit financial audits, demonstrate sound governance, and meet state outcome requirements, including standardized test scores and dropout reporting.[6] Not surprisingly, private schools in the city oppose such constraints on their freedom. Thus far, the Wisconsin legislature has failed to act.

Beyond the lack of accountability, parent information is another weak feature of the Milwaukee plan. Other than terse press releases from the state's Department of Public Instruction, Milwaukee parents have been given little objective information, either about the plan or about the quality of participating schools. ''I don't think any of this was adequately thought through, especially parent information,'' admitted one state official. Professor Witte added, ''We know that over half the parents in Milwaukee don't even know about the choice program.''

Finally, private schools receiving public funds are expected to comply with federal and state nondiscrimination laws. But even here exceptions have been made. In 1990, former U.S. Undersecretary of Education Ted Sanders issued an opinion stating that Milwaukee's private schools did not have to accept disabled youngsters. As a result, in the first year of the program, only nine of the participating students had disabilities. Milwaukee's private schools were thus relieved of the legal obligation to make physical changes in their school buildings, hire new special education teachers, establish individualized programs for the handicapped, and live with the paperwork associated with the federal Education for All Handicapped Children Act—responsibilities and costs that public schools are, by law, required to assume.

The need to confront the crisis in Milwaukee's public schools cannot be denied. Far too many of the city's children are not well served, and it's not surprising that 85 percent of parents taking part in choice said that ''frustration with public schools'' was ''very important'' or ''important'' in their decision to switch their children to private schools. Further, it's encouraging that those participating in the Milwaukee experiment appear to be happy with the way it is working. A majority of students say they feel safe. Few have reported drug or alcohol problems in their new schools. More than 80 percent of the participants believe they are getting a good education. Eighty-four percent of the parents graded the private schools "A" or "B"; only 32 percent felt that way about the public schools.[7]

Much harder to assess, however, is how much and in precisely what ways children have benefited from the change. To explore this essential issue, we visited several of the city's private "choice" schools. We observed that most provided solid instruction in basic skills. But many appeared limited in their ability to match the variety of course offerings in public schools, particularly in the upper grades. Some private schools did have strong music, dance, and foreign-language offerings, but there seemed to be less emphasis on gifted programs, and science equipment was often sparse. On the other hand, private school officials took pride in the large numbers of graduates who pursue post-high school education.

An eighth-grade student told us that her grades rose from Cs and Ds in her former public school to Bs in her new private school: "As soon as I came here it was a big change. Here, teachers care about you. My grades are higher." A seventh-grader told us that she had, for years, attended Milwaukee Public Schools without much success. By her own account: "If you were stuck with a subject like math, the teachers were too busy to help." Worst of all, she said, were the fights: "You really can't avoid it. They'll think you're scared."

For the past two years, both of these students have attended Woodlands School, a tidy but unprepossessing private school in a working class Polish and German neighborhood on the south side of Milwaukee. Here, they enjoy classes of twenty-five pupils or less, each with a teacher and aide, compared with thirty-five students or more in Milwaukee schools. "If you don't understand something," the seventh-grader said, "the teachers take the time, and they care. You don't have to read out of texts all the time. And you don't get pressured into fights." Students interviewed at other private schools echoed these thoughts.

Woodlands, formerly a parochial school, has enrolled thirty-one transfers from the public schools. In contrast to the curriculum and activities they left behind, students at this institution are required to study French starting in kindergarten. A fourth-grade class writes to Irish pen pals. A fourth- and fifth-grade science class has a little incubator for hatching quail eggs. In a seventh- and eighth-grade social studies class, students discuss differences between constitutional government and dictatorship. The teacher in this class took the opportunity to put in a good word for choice: "In a democracy you have the right to choose a private school," she tells her class, "but under a dictatorship you couldn't."

At Harambee Community School, nearly one-third of the 425 students are enrolled under choice. At this school, located in a predominantly black north Milwaukee neighborhood, the emphasis is on skill building and discipline. Students who commit minor infractions like chewing gum or forgetting an assignment risk banishment to a small room in the basement called the "Resource Center." The school now requires uniforms. Fights, drugs, or alcohol use can mean automatic suspension or expulsion. "Our discipline is very, very strict," says principal Dennis Alexander. "But before we punish, they see we care. Still, if you violate the policies here, you're gone."

Harambee requires remedial classes for all children who test low in basic skills. Students must attend classes devoted to single skill areas such as division or multiplication until they "test out." "I brought back basics," says Alexander. "I found that a lot of our 'choice' kids and regular students were lacking them."

The overall climate at "choice" schools was encouraging. Still, on the central issue—educational achievement—standardized test data fail to demonstrate that students who transfer from the public schools are doing any better at private schools. The "choice" students, most of whom were low achievers in the public schools, did move up from the thirtieth to thirty-fourth percentile in nationally normed reading tests in 1991. On the other hand, they declined from the thirty-third to thirtieth percentile in math.[8]

When asked about this lack of progress, private-school officials offered explanations that sounded remarkably like those often heard from their public-school counterparts. "I'm not surprised," said one principal. "We're dealing with issues far beyond the walls of schools. Kids live in places where they don't even have a place to do their homework." Said another: "It doesn't bother me that those tests didn't increase in one year. If the kids stay in the program, I'm confident they'll

70

improve steadily." Still another told us: "Test scores? Nothing should be made of it. Choice students come from economically deprived families. They have discipline problems. They are not already good citizens. They are hard core."

Another disappointing aspect of the Milwaukee program has been the high attrition rate. Of the 562 students who enrolled in private schools in 1991–92, only 311 returned the next year—an attrition rate of more than 40 percent. The reasons for the high rate are unclear—a fact that further serves to illustrate the regulatory vacuum.[9]

Meanwhile, the oft-stated claim that private schools can educate students for half the $5,000 spent by public schools turns out to be misleading. Principals at several of Milwaukee's private schools put their "true cost" per pupil not at the voucher level of $2,600, but closer to $3,000 to $3,500. To close the gap between the state-financed tuition subsidy and the "real" cost, some schools require parents to pledge that they will engage in extensive fund-raising and volunteer work. Those who fail to fulfill this obligation may be assessed extra tuition, or have their children expelled. "Whereas public schools have to hire lunch aides and other school workers, free parent labor amounts to a very sizable subsidy for private schools," says Professor Witte.

Participating private schools also get considerable help from businesses and foundations. Harambee School, for example, receives about $50,000 monthly from the Jane and Lloyd Pettit Foundation. The Bradley Foundation also contributes generously to several Milwaukee "choice" schools.

However, the most important private-school subsidy comes from teachers themselves, through low salaries and limited benefits. In 1991–92, Milwaukee public school teachers' salaries ranged from $23,113 for beginners with bachelor's degrees to $46,907 for veterans with master's degrees. By contrast, teachers at the city's private "choice" schools earned from $11,500 to $27,000. What accounts for this? First, many of the private schools were formerly parochial schools; hence, some of the teachers and administrative staff are members of religious orders. At Urban Day, for example, three of sixteen teachers are nuns. Second, roughly one-third of the teachers at these schools are young and at the lower end of the salary scale. Finally, many private-school teachers are willing and able, because of family circumstances, to trade off high wages for attractive working conditions: "I felt a certain friendliness here, a feeling. We are allowed a tremendous amount of freedom," said one science and math teacher who formerly taught in the suburbs but now teaches at a Milwaukee private school for "quite a bit less money."

Thus, Milwaukee's young, limited plan gives us at least some insights into the potential and the problems of private-school choice. On the positive side, a majority of children who participate feel happier and safer. Most parents are highly satisfied. And yet, more than 40 percent of children who originally enrolled did not continue. In addition, test scores and other data have yet to show that private schools can produce higher achievement among children.

Private schools insist, with some justification, that two years isn't much time for judging results, and that "choice" students who remain in their programs will end up better off than they would have at public schools. But that remains to be seen. Accountability is virtually nonexistent, and repeated claims by advocates of the voucher system that Milwaukee private schools do the same job for half the money have proven to be questionable.

Especially discouraging is the fact that Milwaukee's inadequate system of parent information has left most families in the dark about the "choice" plan. Many parents can't even find out about their options, much less exercise them. Surveys reveal that the most educated parents are most actively involved. It also should be noted, once again, that children with disabilities can be excluded.

As to its larger impact, it appears that the Milwaukee plan has, to date, neither helped nor hurt the city's public schools. Financially, only about $750,000 out of $243.8 million in state aid in 1991–92 has been diverted from public to private schools.[10] Still, though the cost in dollars may be small, the program's very existence conveys the message that Milwaukee's public school problems are almost intractable.

Many of those most closely involved with Milwaukee's program view it as a signal that time is running out for the city's schools to make fundamental changes. In the words of Jeannette Mitchell, Milwaukee's school board president: "As a board, we recognize that right now choice may not be a big deal. But choice is one more thing that says we should get better. . . . We feel we have a window of opportunity of about two years to get results and get back support.''

Tom Fonfara, Governor Thompson's aide, sees indications that choice in Milwaukee has nudged the state's education community toward acceptance of school reform ideas: ''It is incredibly interesting to me that the teacher unions and school board associations are now saying that they don't want to be perceived as a roadblock to reform.'' By contrast, Dick Collins, president of the Wisconsin Education Association Council, which tried unsuccessfully to block the plan in court, argues that choice ''takes off the pressure to change things. It gives the legislature an excuse not to do anything. They can argue that they've done something.''

Given the Milwaukee plan's limited impact, why do so many educators still object to this modest local experiment, which involves only several hundred thousand tax dollars and serves only several hundred students? The reasons become a bit clearer when the plan is described in less benign terms. What the state of Wisconsin has done, one critic charges, is to direct state tax dollars formerly used to support a large city public school district to a ''duplicate, competitive private system of schools'' that operates largely free of state accountability or regulation.[11]

Whatever else may be said of it, Milwaukee's plan has failed to demonstrate that vouchers can, in and of themselves, spark school improvement. A few students have been enabled to leave the city's public schools, and they feel pleased with the decision they have made. But no evidence can be found that the participating students made significant academic advances or that either the public or private schools have been revitalized by the transfers. Further, Milwaukee simply does not have enough nonsectarian private schools willing or able to participate in the voucher plan to make much difference to the vast majority of children.

In Milwaukee, then, the battle lines have been drawn as clearly as any place in the nation between those who believe that public education cannot improve without the threat of competition, and those who believe that a voucher system would weaken public schools and dramatically reduce the prospects that such renewal ever will occur.

# CHAPTER 6

## *In Search of Common Ground*

S CHOOL CHOICE can no longer be dismissed as an arcane textbook theory. It has emerged in recent years as an aggressively promoted centerpiece of education reform. Thirteen states and scores of districts have adopted some form of choice. Successes have been noted. Yet our examination of the choice "landscape"—from Milwaukee, Wisconsin, to East Harlem, New York, and from Minnesota to Massachusetts—leads us to conclude that this strategy is not the key to widespread school improvement.

Choice, at its best, empowers parents, stimulates teachers to be more creative and, most important, gives students a new sense of attachment to their schools and to learning. We saw such achievements in school districts across the country—programs where choice has truly made a difference. On the other hand, the negative impact of selected statewide choice programs on impoverished urban districts such as Brockton and Gloucester, Massachusetts, as well as tiny rural ones like Motley, Minnesota, and Exira, Iowa, cannot be ignored. Neither can we forget that, in Milwaukee, the promise of private-school choice has, to date, outdistanced the performance.

Clearly, a myth has grown up around choice. The assumption is that the competition of the marketplace will strengthen good schools while forcing weak ones either to shape up or be closed down. The reality is, though, that parents pick schools for a variety of reasons. It is, therefore, difficult to see how moving students from one school to another will, in and of itself, renew public education. Other factors surely are involved, and it's a diversion to present choice as a panacea—some grand design that can sweep away all difficulties that impede schools and restrict learning.

Prof. Nathan Glazer, in a thoughtful review of the constructive changes in East Harlem, correctly acknowledges that choice was crucial. But there was something deeper. "Choice," writes Glazer, "was the term selected to describe the character of the revolution in East Harlem, but parental choice was only part of the story. Indeed, the story begins with educational innovations rather than choice, which was entailed only because the innovations had to find students on which to try their ideas. A key characteristic of the innovations was that they came from the teachers, not from top administrators."[1]

The time has come, therefore, to move beyond the school-choice rhetoric and begin to shape a more comprehensive approach to school renewal—to search for common ground. It is time for educators on both sides of the debate to focus not so much on school *location* but on student *learning*. And the first step, we believe, is to diagnose, with accuracy, the problem. Just why are so many schools unable to deliver on their promise? Why do so many students fail to learn?

The evidence is overwhelming that the crises in education relate not just to school governance but to pathologies that surround the schools. The harsh truth is that, in many communities, the family is a far more imperiled institution than the school, and teachers are being asked to do what parents have not been able to accomplish. Today, the nation's public schools are called upon to stop drugs, reduce teenage pregnancy, feed students, improve health, and eliminate gang violence, while still meeting academic standards. And if they fail anywhere along the line we condemn them for not meeting our high-minded expectations.

Consider, once again, District 4. In this poverty-ridden section of New York City, more than half the children come from homes headed by single parents. Almost 80 percent are eligible for the free lunch program. Years ago, school choice brought a new sense of energy and creativity to this district. Yet, even today, far too many students are academically deficient, and District 4 schools still struggle against almost overwhelming odds. Even with the positive influence of school choice, is it realistic to expect an island of academic excellence in a sea of social crises?

Simply stated, educational excellence relates not just to schools but to communities as well. Writing in the *Wall Street Journal*, Robert Carr declares: "The problems of America's schools stem in large part from

76

causes deep in the national experience: urban blight, drugs, the erosion of the family, and long-standing failure to direct sufficient resources to the schools. In the face of these pressures, the schools have been called upon to take over roles formerly played by the family, churches, and other agencies, ranging from sex education to housing and feeding children from dawn to dusk, well beyond school hours."[2]

Consider also that many problems adversely affecting the education of children begin very early, even before birth itself. Last year, in a Carnegie Foundation survey, kindergarten teachers reported that one-third of their students come to school not well prepared to learn because of poor health, inadequate nurturing, and language deprivation. A more recent survey identified lack of parental support, child abuse, poor nutrition, violence, and drug problems as serious detriments to learning.[3] How tragic it would be if the school choice debate shifted attention away from these pathologies that harm children, weaken schools, and tear at the very fabric of the nation.

If we are truly serious about better education, the time has come to launch a national effort on behalf of children. It's time to acknowledge the interrelatedness of the home, health clinics, preschools, the workplace—all of the institutions and social forces that influence children's lives. What we need are inspired leadership, a sense of urgency, and, above all, the will to create a better life for children so that all will come to school well prepared to learn.

It's also time to reaffirm public education and commit ourselves to having a school of quality within the reach of every child. Many schools are struggling, and some are failing, but others are dramatically successful. Further, thousands of teachers are performing heroic acts every single day, and it's dishonest and dishonorable to ignore these heroic efforts. Instead of bashing schools, let's celebrate success and build on the good practices now in place.

For years, the U.S. Department of Education has named Blue Ribbon Schools from coast to coast. Literally hundreds of public schools have received national recognition. And in our own travels, we found many schools where the spirit of renewal is pervasive.

Jackson-Keller Elementary School in San Antonio, Texas, serves an ethnically diverse, poor, highly mobile student population. In 1985 the school was forced to shut down due to declining enrollment. But it reopened three years later with an innovative "integrated curriculum." By developing a strong partnership with parents, Jackson-Keller has achieved a new sense of community mission, steadily improving test scores, and an amazing 97-percent daily attendance rate. "The secret of renewal," summarizes principal Alicia Thomas, "is not vouchers or choice. It's devising your own agenda. It's about a school community reaching down within itself to find its mission, and then working to achieve it."

The setting could hardly be more different at the Orchard School, which serves 220 children in the upscale suburb of Ridgewood, New Jersey. This school might easily have rested complacently on its laurels with standardized test scores in the upper 90th percentile. Instead, a committee of teachers, parents, and the principal spent summer months and hundreds of weeknight hours devising the "Orchard 2000 Plan," which has led the school community into a dramatic re-evaluation of philosophy, curriculum, teaching, and student grading. The aim is to go well beyond traditional elementary school content and have every child at Orchard become a self-directed problem-solver and adept communicator.

The spirit of school reform also might have bypassed New Suncook, an elementary school in Lovell, Maine. Despite the rural setting, principal Gary MacDonald has made sure that his school is anything but isolated. In 1988 and 1989, he and several teachers flew to Seattle, at their own expense, to meet school reformers and attend education conventions. Today, New Suncook has restructured itself, grouping kindergartners through second-graders in five independent units within the school. The school also disbanded special education classes and integrated all disabled children into regular classes.

These are but a few of the literally hundreds of public schools where the spirit of renewal has arisen not from the threat of competition but rather from their own commitment to improve. Achieving genuine national reform remains, of course, a work in progress. Still, we are convinced that neighborhood schools like New Suncook, Orchard, Jackson-Keller, and thousands of others offer daily proof that revitalization can, in the end, come from the simple act of parents and professionals working together toward common goals.

We do not suggest that all is well in public education. Some schools *are* failing. Some children *are* shockingly ill-served, and it would be foolish, indeed wholly irresponsible, to insist that what we have today should go unchallenged. Excellence in education for all students remains the key to America's civic and economic future, and indeed, it is this goal that brings advocates and adversaries of choice together. The conflict appears to be not over ends but over means, and the time has come, we believe, for all educators, regardless of their position on school choice, to join in common cause.

What we propose is a national strategy for renewal that affirms the neighborhood school tradition, while also expanding opportunities for mobility and enrichment. This approach surely would include a commitment to early education, with small classes and a focus on basic skills. It would include breaking up large schools into smaller units, and making all schools into places where there is active, not passive, learning. It would involve parents as partners in the process. And it surely would include high academic standards and accountability.

Above all, this new strategy must ensure that teachers are empowered. This is truly at the heart of the school choice debate. The issue isn't whether students are free to move from school to school, but whether decision making can be shifted to the local level. Indeed, advocates of school choice are quite right to remind us that many schools are caught in a web of regulations, and that teachers are often held responsible for the bureaucratic rather than the educational aspects of their work.

In confronting this bureaucratic gridlock, some districts have successfully used "choice" as the means to empower teachers. In other places, decision making has been decentralized within the traditional neighborhood school arrangement. Kentucky, for example, has actually mandated local decision making. Under a recent school reform law, every school must establish, by 1996, a school-based decision-making council consisting of two parents, three teachers, and the principal. Each council will have authority over the budget, instructional materials, school management, curriculum, and other school affairs. Already, six hundred of the state's thirteen hundred public schools have such councils.

Change is also beginning in individual districts. St. Paul, Minnesota; Cherry Valley outside Denver, Colorado; and Lansing, Michigan, are among a growing number of districts working to give local schools more control. One of the boldest initiatives is in Moses Lake, Washington. For the past four years, that district's thirteen schools have been given nearly total control over supply and contract money, special-education funds, Chapter 1 aid, and certain state funds. The philosophy of the district is to turn the organizational chart upside down, putting the district's fifty-six hundred students at the top, and the superintendent and school board at the bottom, in a support role.

What is clear is this: Until local schools have a meaningful level of autonomy, we simply will not have a real test of what is possible in education. There is, however, a related matter. High academic standards also are essential. Indeed, holding local schools accountable is perhaps the most important and most neglected part of public education today. The focus of such accountability should be on outcomes. What is needed, we believe, is a report card on every school, one that includes a wide range of measures related to school goals and procedures as well as student progress.

Specifically, we recommend that each school be asked to demonstrate, at regular intervals, the educational effectiveness of its program. Such a strategy might include information on students' academic progress, attendance, graduation rates, school climate, parent participation, and curriculum standards. After a reasonable period, if a school fails to provide evidence that it is giving its students a quality education, an external School Evaluation Team should intervene. The review team might conclude that a school had poor leadership and recommend that a new principal be brought in. It might assign a resident advisor to the school to clarify goals and renew the program. As a last resort, the school might be closed and reopened with better leadership and a new education plan. The team might even conclude that a failing school was underfunded and recommend emergency state aid. After all, account-ability means holding state legislatures as well as schools responsible.

But where does school choice fit into this equation?

We conclude that in this new school reform strategy, districtwide choice has a place. It can, under the right circumstances, help revitalize schools, empower teachers and principals, and stimulate parents to con-sider which program is best suited for their children. But, before choice is introduced, every school in the district must be a school worth choos-ing. It's simply not fair to have a few attractive "magnets" or "charter schools" which serve a handful of students while neglecting the rest. School choice, in other words, must be viewed as a way to *supplement,* not *supplant,* the network of local schools.

Further, for a districtwide "choice" program to be effective, par-ents must be actively engaged. Indeed, if parent empowerment is an important goal of school choice, parents might well be asked whether they want the program in the first place. Parents also must be fully informed about the alternatives available to them, and special efforts must surely be made to reach the least advantaged. Finally, transporta-tion must be provided to students who might not otherwise be able to get to their preferred school. Choice within a district has no meaning if the desired school is beyond reach.

A program such as the one we've just described may fit nicely into a community where schools are concentrated and where students can move conveniently from one place to another. But what struck us so forcefully during our study is that choice is, because of location, a wholly unrealistic proposal for literally millions of families. For many, there is simply no other school within easy reach, or if there is, the alternative school may be no better than the one close by. The solution, we believe, is to focus choice not on a *building* but on *quality educa-tion.* Instead of providing choice only *among* schools, why not create choices *within* schools?

Advocates of choice are correct in stressing that we must return the learner to the center of the enterprise. But if the true goal of "choice" is to discover the best fit between the educational process and the student, then we regard choice within a school as distilling this central aim and injecting it into every single institution.

Few places better illustrate our choice-within-schools idea than South Mountain, a neighborhood high school in Phoenix, Arizona. In 1988, South Mountain was just another struggling school in that city's toughest section, known mainly for violence and a dropout rate approaching 25 percent. With the help of desegregation funds, the thirty-three hundred student institution divided itself into five speciality schools: visual arts, performing arts, aerospace, law, and mass communications. The resulting ''South Mountain Plan,'' now in its fifth year, also completely restructured the school day so that teachers spend half their time tutoring, making home visits, and calling parents.

South Mountain sees itself as a full-range community and social service center, operating a drug-prevention and social-work program right on campus. Academic standards have also been toughened: all freshmen, for example, are now required to take algebra. All of this has paid off handsomely: the dropout rate has been cut by more than half, to 10.9 percent, violence is rare, and the school is gaining some three hundred students a year. As a result, South Mountain has been cited by the state as one of the top five high schools in Arizona. ''Our school sees itself as a hub of activity for the parents and the community,'' says principal Art Lebowitz. ''It's almost a city within a city.''

What we propose in the school choice debate, then, is a search for common ground—a plan for school renewal on which all educators might agree. The stakes are far too high for policy makers and school leaders to divide into warring camps, driven more by ideology than by ideas. It is possible, we believe, to break the bureaucratic gridlock and to extend the educational options for parents and students while still affirming the neighborhood school tradition and making every school a school worth choosing.

# CHAPTER 7

## *School Choice in Perspective*

W HILE REFLECTING on the current school-choice debate, we were impressed by just how little attention is being given to the history of public education or to the large body of thought about the role of schooling in building a democratic nation. We are, after all, not the first generation to address issues of education policy. One hundred and sixty years ago, young Abraham Lincoln of Illinois described education as "the most important subject which we as a people can be engaged in."[1] We believe, then, that it is essential to consider the ideas of the past as we shape educational policy for the future. The alternative is to grapple with crucial issues in a historical and intellectual void and allow high-decibel rhetoric to substitute for reason.

The nation's public schools have been one of America's most responsive institutions. As early as 1647, the Massachusetts Bay Colony required that all towns and villages of fifty or more citizens hire a schoolmaster to teach all children to read and write. Even in that day, it was expected that citizens in each community, *working together,* would assume responsibility for the education of children. Guided by this grassroots approach to education, we have built, here in the United States, a network of eighty-three thousand public schools from Presque Isle, Maine, to the Islands of Hawaii, serving forty-two million students in classrooms every single day. Let us acknowledge, then, that the public schools, with all their failings, are still one of America's most remarkable achievements. Without question, the success of every student must be the central concern of education.

Still, a point of special concern to us is that school choice arguments are often framed almost exclusively in terms of the alleged benefits to individuals. This one-sided approach to educational policy, one that stresses only the *private* benefits of schooling, departs sharply from a vast body of work by well-regarded thinkers and writers underscoring the social imperatives of education and recognizing that schools also promote *the common good*. Philanthropist David Rockefeller, Jr., captured the point precisely: "The emphasis on choice seems premised on the benefits that education confers on individuals, not on society, whereas the genius of American public education is premised on its recognition of schooling's communal and civic purposes."[2]

More than half a century ago, Merle Curti's pathbreaking *Social Ideas of American Educators* impressively documented the thesis that the formation of a sense of identification with and obligation to the larger society was fundamental to the American pedagogical enterprise from the beginning. When the American Philosophical Society of Philadelphia sponsored an essay contest in 1795 to devise an American system of education, Curti tells us, the essays almost uniformly stressed the importance of building a school system that would promote common national purposes and "inculcate in the youth of America loyalty to its institutions, purposes, and ideals."[3]

Thomas Jefferson, the nation's first "education president," called it the duty of the state to establish laws for educating the common people. "Education . . . ," wrote our third president, "engrafts a new man on the native stock, and improves what in his nature was vicious and perverse into qualities of virtue and social worth." With the help of public education, Jefferson said grandly, "tyranny and oppressions of body and mind will vanish like evil spirits at the dawn of day."[4]

Of course, practice did not live up to theory; it rarely does. Still, statesmen in the early republic did take seriously the task of stirring in children a sense of mutual social obligation and common citizenship. It was understood that educators had a democratic mission. And this was to be accomplished not just by the subject matter taught but by the simple fact that public schools were a community enterprise, with citizens in each neighborhood working together to advance the education of their children.

Alexis de Tocqueville's classic study of the United States in the 1830s, *Democracy in America,* stressed the key role of the public schools in shaping an American national identity and in helping to counteract divisive class differences in the emerging society. Another

84

French visitor of that period, Michael Chevalier, made the sweeping claim that, thanks to the public schools and other agencies influencing the national character, "the American mass has reached a much higher degree of initiation [in public affairs] than the European mass, for it does not need to be governed; every man here [in the United States] has in himself the principle of self-government in a much higher degree and is more fit to take a part in public affairs."[5]

Horace Mann, the most influential American educator of the antebellum years, repeatedly returned to this theme in the well-known series of reports he issued in the 1830s and 1840s as secretary of the state board of education in the Commonwealth of Massachusetts. In 1845, for example, Mann wrote: "As each citizen is to participate in the power of governing others, it is an essential preliminary that he should be imbued with a feeling for the wants, and a sense of the rights, of those whom he is chosen to govern. . . . It becomes, then, a momentous question, whether the children in our schools are educated in reference to themselves and their private interests only, or with a regard to the great social duties and prerogatives that await them in afterlife."[6]

Franklin D. Roosevelt, in a letter dated July 26, 1939, also affirmed the democratic function of education: "Everyone knows that democracy cannot long stand unless its foundation is kept constantly reinforced through the processes of education. . . . Education for democracy cannot merely be taken for granted. What goes on in the schools every hour of the day, on the playground and in the classroom, whether reflecting methods of control by the teacher, or opportunities for self-expression by pupils, must be checked against the fact that the children are growing up to live in a democracy. That the schools make worthy citizens is the most important responsibility placed upon them."

The premier historian of education in our day, the late Lawrence Cremin, made the same point in his magisterial study of American education. Throughout the twentieth century, writes Cremin in the concluding volume of his study, American schools have "tended to portray themselves, and in turn to be perceived as, community institutions; indeed, the very fact of their being educative institutions seemed to constitute them as *community* institutions."[7]

We do not suggest that the ideas of these scholars and public leaders should be embraced without discussion and debate. In their more lofty rhetorical flights, school advocates often overstated the potential of the public schools to create a sense of civic loyalty and to moderate the extremes of individualism. Some, caught up in the enthusiasm of their social vision, downplayed the other, equally important function of public education: to provide each pupil with the tools to achieve his or her individual goals.

Nor are we contending that American public education ever completely fulfilled the social role the theorists envisioned. The long, shameful history of racial discrimination in the schools would alone be enough to refute any such naive claim. Our argument here is not about past educational practice, but about past educational thought—and about the need to draw upon that thought as we confront the issues of today.

Obviously, the proponents of school choice are not oblivious to the social dimensions of public education; nor do they consciously wish to destroy this function in their enthusiasm for change. No doubt most advocates of choice would readily agree that the mission of schools includes both individual intellectual development and community empowerment.

The fact remains, however, that in the current debate, public education often is disparaged, its history neglected. Arguments for choice are stated in the vocabulary of individual self-interest, while downgrading the ways in which our vision of public education, including the neighborhood-school arrangement, has served larger social ends. Adopting the language of the marketplace, education is portrayed as a solitary act of consumerism. Under systems of choice, advocates say, one can shop around for a school, much as one shops for a VCR or a new car. The purpose of the enterprise, we are told, is to satisfy ''the customer.''

To frame the issue in these terms is to distort the vision of public education beyond recognition. From the very first it was understood that the nation's schools should serve both private benefit and the public good. And this was to be accomplished, at least in part, by the way we organized our schools. Local citizens joined together to build schools and hire schoolmasters, and the very fact that children from a wide range of social and economic backgrounds came together in the common school richly enhanced the dimensions of public education. The schools were social anchors and served the ideals of the nation.

Today, however, the vision of community—of shared purposes and goals—has rapidly eroded. In *Habits of the Heart: Individualism and Commitment in American Life*, University of California sociologist Robert N. Bellah and associates echo de Tocqueville's warning of 150 years earlier. They decry an individualism so rampant that each person would be "shut up in the solitude of his own heart."[8] Bellah writes: "We are concerned that this individualism may have grown cancerous . . . that it may be destroying the survival of freedom itself." He suggests the challenge of learning from "those cultural traditions and practices that, without destroying individuality, serve to limit and restrain the destructive side of individualism and provide alternative models for how Americans might live."[9]

As Americans seek to recapture "a moral language that will transcend . . . radical individualism,"[10] they would do well to reexamine classical republican ideology, with its emphasis on the sense of common interests and obligations—the awareness of a shared citizenship—that can make disparate individuals into a unified people. Historically, no institution has been more central to transmitting this tradition than the public school.

More than ever before, this nation must reaffirm public education, especially in our disadvantaged neighborhoods. In these pockets of poverty and neglect, libraries have closed, churches have fled to the suburbs, health clinics have been abandoned. Yet, the public school—flawed and under siege—still opens its doors every weekday morning. It is perhaps the only institution within reach that offers hope. Rather than talk of closing schools, then, we should talk about expanding services, and about giving neighborhood schools the resources they need not only to empower students, but to renew neighborhoods as well.

Here, then, is the essential point. The school-choice debate is best pursued, we believe, not by brandishing unexamined ideological slogans. Nor is it advanced by accumulating endless data and statistics, important as these are. Rather, we must enlarge the discussion to focus on the goals of public education. Participants in the discourse must begin to extend their intellectual reach backward in time, and outward from the lone individual to society. We must draw from the full, complex history that has informed the American educational enterprise, and not single out one strand of that discourse.

The world of Thomas Jefferson and Horace Mann is not our world. Still, the nation's public schools collectively remain one of America's most vital institutions, with the mission of sustaining a democratic nation as well as serving the individual. When all is said and done, we dare not permit the current debate about choice to blur this vision. The goal must be to make every public school a source of national strength in pursuit of *excellence for all*.

We must choose nothing less.

# APPENDICES

# APPENDIX A

## *Survey of Parents with Children Attending Public Schools, 1992*

Table 1

Approximately How Far Is It to the
School Your Child Attended Last Year?

| | |
|---|---|
| Less than 2 miles | 47% |
| 2 to 4.99 miles | 27 |
| 5 to 9.99 miles | 16 |
| 10 miles or more | 10 |

Table 2

What Form of Transportation Did
Your Child Usually Use to Get to School?

| | |
|---|---|
| Walk or bicycle | 16% |
| Car or carpool | 35 |
| School bus | 43 |
| Public transportation | 2 |
| Combination | 3 |
| Other | 1 |

Table 3

How Long Did It Take Your Child to Get to School?

| | |
|---|---|
| Less than 10 minutes | 34% |
| 10 - 19 minutes | 34 |
| 20 - 29 minutes | 11 |
| 30 minutes or more | 21 |

## Table 4

### How Satisfied Are You With the Quality of the Education Your Child Got at This School Last Year?

| | |
|---|---|
| Very satisfied | 51% |
| Somewhat satisfied | 36 |
| Somewhat dissatisfied | 8 |
| Very dissatisfied | 5 |
| Don't know | 1 |

## Table 5

### In Your Opinion, Has the Quality of Education at Your Child's School Been Getting Better or Worse, or Has It Stayed about the Same?

| | |
|---|---|
| Getting better | 30% |
| Getting worse | 15 |
| Stayed the same | 48 |
| Don't know | 7 |

## Table 6

### Approximately How Far Is It to the Next Closest Public School with Your Child's Grade Level?

| | |
|---|---|
| Less than 2 miles | 25% |
| 2 to 4.99 miles | 26 |
| 5 to 9.99 miles | 24 |
| 10 miles or more | 25 |

## Table 7

### Would You Like to Enroll Your Child in the Next Closest School?

| | |
|---|---|
| Yes | 14% |
| No | 83 |
| Don't know | 3 |

## Table 8

### Let's Assume That You Could Enroll Your Child in This Next Closest School. What Form of Transportation Would Your Child Use to Get There?

| | |
|---|---|
| Walk or bicycle | 14% |
| Car or carpool | 40 |
| School bus | 38 |
| Public transportation | 3 |
| Combination | 2 |
| Other | 1 |
| None available | 1 |
| Don't know | 1 |

## Table 9

### If No Other Transportation Was Available, Could You Personally Arrange to Get Your Child to This Next Closest School at Your Own Expense?

| | |
|---|---|
| Yes | 87% |
| No | 11 |
| Don't know | 2 |

## Table 10

### Is There Some Other School to Which You Would Like to Send Your Child? This School Could Be Public or Private, Inside or Outside of Your District, with Your Child's Grade Level.

| | |
|---|---|
| Yes, public school | 9% |
| Yes, private school | 19 |
| No | 70 |
| Don't know | 2 |

## Table 11

### Approximately How Far Is It to This Other School?

| | |
|---|---|
| Less than 2 miles | 16% |
| 2 to 4.99 miles | 18 |
| 5 to 9.99 miles | 25 |
| 10 miles or more | 41 |

## Table 12

### Let's Assume That You Could Enroll Your Child in This Other School. What Form of Transportation Would Your Child Use To Get There?

| | |
|---|---|
| Walk or bicycle | 1% |
| Car or carpool | 64 |
| School bus | 18 |
| Public transportation | 7 |
| Combination | 1 |
| Other | 3 |
| None available | 3 |
| Don't know | 3 |

## Table 13

### If No Other Transportation Was Available, Could You Personally Arrange to Get Your Child to This Other School at Your Expense?

| | |
|---|---|
| Yes | 83% |
| No | 15 |
| Don't know | 2 |

## Table 14

### Some People Think That Parents Should Be Given a Voucher Which They Could Use Toward Enrolling Their Child in a Private School at Public Expense. Do You Support or Oppose That Idea?

| | |
|---|---|
| Support | 32% |
| Oppose | 62 |
| Don't know | 6 |

# Survey of Public Opinion, 1992

## Table 1

Please imagine two people having a discussion on how to improve the public schools in this country. Mr. Smith says: The best way to improve education is to focus directly on supporting neighborhood schools, giving every school the resources needed to achieve excellence. Mr. Jones says: The best way to improve education is to let schools compete with each other for students. Quality schools would be further strengthened and weak schools would improve or close.

Who are you more likely to agree with, Mr. Smith, who would support every neighborhood school, or Mr. Jones, who would let schools compete for students?

| | |
|---|---|
| Mr. Smith | 82% |
| Mr. Jones | 15 |
| No opinion | 2 |
| Don't know/No response | 1 |

# APPENDIX C

## *Survey of Chief State School Officers, 1992*

### ALABAMA

The 1991 Educational Improvement Act allows any of the state's 129 districts to participate in inter- and intradistrict choice. Long-standing magnet-school programs exist in Mobile, Jefferson, and Montgomery Counties, and in Huntsville. The "choice" plan is optional for all districts. Any two systems can agree to a plan but must file it with the state board. As of July, no districts had done so. State officials predict limited impact due to court-ordered desegregation plans, the large number of systems with only one high school, and the lack of additional funding for transportation.

### ALASKA

A "Governor's Commission on School Choice" issued a report in the summer of 1992 proposing a three-year pilot program authorizing charter schools, expanding opportunities for cross-district student transfers, and establishing a postsecondary options program allowing high school students to attend college courses for credit. Gov. Walter Hickel had asked the commission to study the feasibility of a statewide voucher plan to include private-school choice, but the commission rejected the idea. The panel's recommendations will be discussed at public forums this fall, and the state board will make final recommendations to the legislature sometime thereafter.

### ARIZONA

Open enrollment exists on wide scale, but is left to the discretion of local districts. Since 1984, the state has allowed high school students to take college courses not offered at their high school. The legislature considered but failed to adopt a statewide "choice" plan in the 1992 session. Some 9,000 of the state's 683,000 public school students attended school outside their districts as of March, while another 21,000 attended non-neighborhood schools in their own districts. Over 78 percent of the state's districts enroll non-resident students. A state survey of parents found that two-thirds of the students who made inter- and intra-district transfers were white. Only one-third cited academics as the reason for switching schools.

## ARKANSAS

Statewide choice was enacted in 1989 and amended in 1991. Currently 1,667 students—about .4 percent of the state's 430,000 public school pupils—are taking part in interdistrict transfers. District participation is optional. Districts can limit the number of students they accept depending on the space available, the impact on class size, or the effect on existing desegregation plans. Parents are responsible for transporting students to the border of the receiving district. Transferring students are ineligible for interscholastic sports for one year.

## CALIFORNIA

In 1992, legislators considered a statewide interdistrict measure allowing more freedom to transfer among public schools. A second proposal would open the way to state-funded transfers to private schools beginning in 1993. Neither has been adopted. In July 1992, a statewide voucher initiative was ruled off the November 1992 ballot by the state supreme court due to the lack of validated signatures, but it's widely assumed that backers will try again for the June 1994 ballot. If enacted, this initiative would offer all pupils a "scholarship" equal to 50 percent of local and state per-pupil costs, spendable at any public or private school.

Since 1987 the state's education code has allowed parents to enroll their children in the district in which they work. Some 15,000 to 20,000 students are enrolled under this option. Many others are involved in local inter- and intradistrict choice programs.

## COLORADO

Some five thousand students participate in a range of "choice" options, and 134 of 176 school districts have open enrollment for outside students, depending mainly on space considerations. Colorado's 1990 "Interdistrict Public Schools of Choice Pilot Program" awards up to $100,000 to participating districts. Other options: a "Second Chance" program enacted in 1985 allowing dropouts to attend any school in or out of their district, at state expense; and a Postsecondary Enrollment Options program allowing eleventh- and twelfth-graders to take college courses at public universities. A plan to include private universities is under consideration.

In November, voters rejected by a two-to-one margin a citizen initiative that would have provided up to $2,500 in public funds to parents sending their children to private or parochial school or educating their children at home.

## CONNECTICUT

The state is using startup grants to encourage "regional" magnet-school programs aimed at promoting urban-suburban student transfers to achieve racial balance. By 1992 only one such magnet existed, in East Lyme. The state also contains seventeen intradistrict magnet schools mostly in urban districts.

## DELAWARE

The "choice" debate has not led to statewide action as yet.

## DISTRICT OF COLUMBIA

In the summer of 1992 Superintendent Franklin L. Smith proposed a controlled "choice" plan to convert every public school in the district

101

into a magnet school within five years and allow parents to choose among them.

## FLORIDA

In the 1992 session, the legislature rejected a statewide plan providing choice "certificates" redeemable at any public school, or grants to low-income families at eligible private schools. Charlotte County has had an open enrollment policy for years, and many districts operate magnet-school programs. Since 1987, the state has had a postsecondary options plan allowing qualified high school students to enroll in community college courses.

## GEORGIA

The state has no law authorizing choice, but does permit non-resident transfers for "compelling reasons."

## HAWAII

Hawaii does not have statewide "choice," but parents may apply for a "geographic exception" that would allow their children to go to schools outside their attendance area, as long as both the sending and receiving schools agree.

## IDAHO

An open enrollment law was adopted by the state in 1990. According to a statewide survey, some 2,580 students attended schools outside their home districts during the 1990–91 school year, up 20 percent from the preceding year. Local superintendents surveyed said remoteness and lack of space limited participation.

## ILLINOIS

There are no statewide "choice" plans or initiatives here at present. A plan to pay up to $2,300 per child in state money to help Chicago parents send children to private schools was not approved by the legislature. A policy study in 1990 supported local "choice" initiatives but declined to recommend statewide open enrollment because of widespread disparities in local funding. Several districts including Carpentersville and Kankakee have districtwide plans. Rockford and Waukegan are developing comprehensive "controlled choice" programs, and Chicago has operated magnet schools for years.

## INDIANA

Lawmakers have rejected several open enrollment plans, pilot programs for various "choice" options, and a public-private school voucher program. The Indianapolis school board in 1992 approved a "controlled choice" plan, breaking the district into zones with equal minority populations and allowing options for elementary and middle school students. The plan is on hold pending court approval. Critics including teachers and community leaders have denounced it as a hastily drafted response to a voucher program funded privately by the Indianapolis-based Golden Rule Insurance Co. that allows poor inner city children to attend private or parochial schools.

## IOWA

In 1991–92, some 5,000 students participated in a statewide "choice" plan enacted in 1989. Another two thousand are expected to participate in the fall of 1992. All districts must participate, but transfers can be limited in the dozen districts with desegregation plans. State aid follows students, and the state subsidizes transportation for poor students. Transfer students had been required to wait one year before participating in interscholastic athletics, but the legislature reduced this waiting period to 90 days. A state survey of parents found a high level of satisfaction with choice. The typical family taking part in choice was white, had above-average family income and education, and was transferring from a smaller district to a larger one with more course offerings or extracurricular activities. The four main reasons for transfers were, in order: general education benefits, family convenience, values and philosophy, and nearness to home.

103

## KANSAS

No statewide open enrollment laws are under active consideration. Students can transfer at the discretion of participating districts, and some 6,500 attend schools outside their districts.

## KENTUCKY

Several statewide "choice" measures died in the legislature this year. One would have allowed students to attend any public school in the state but required them to provide their own transportation.

## LOUISIANA

Numerous school choice bills have died in the legislature in recent years, including some permitting private-school participation. But the state has a number of magnet schools, programs for gifted and talented pupils, and a postsecondary options program for high-achieving high school students.

## MAINE

No statewide plan exists at present, though individual schools allow student transfers. The rural nature of the state and thus the high transportation costs make widespread choice difficult. For years the state has allowed public funds to follow students to nonreligious private schools if public schools are unavailable in their home districts. In 1987 the legislature adopted a postsecondary options plan allowing high school students to attend colleges for credit, with tuition paid by their district.

## MARYLAND

Maryland has no statewide choice plan, but since 1985 Prince Georges County has had an extensive magnet-school program as a result of desegregation.

## MASSACHUSETTS

A statewide "choice" plan that took effect September 1991 permits interdistrict transfer by any student, provided that the receiving district agrees. Participation is optional for all districts, though none can bar its own students from leaving. About 30 districts opted into the plan in its first year, and 1,100 students took part. As originally adopted, the plan required a transferring student's home district to reimburse the receiving district for the full per-pupil cost. The legislature amended the law in July 1992 to cap reimbursements at $5,000 per pupil, but the law remains among the nation's most punitive. The state also has highly acclaimed intradistrict "controlled choice" programs in Cambridge, Boston, Lawrence, and Fall River.

## MICHIGAN

A statewide "choice" program was to take effect in the 1992–93 school year, but the legislature decided in 1992 to postpone it for a year because budgetary problems left the state unable to provide needed transportation aid. The plan, which will be mandatory for all districts in the 1993–94 school year, requires every district with more than one school at a particular grade level to develop and implement a school choice plan. Local plans must provide, among other things, adequate transportation and parent information about available programs. Districts failing to do so stand to lose state funding.

## MINNESOTA

Widely regarded as a pioneer of choice, Minnesota has had strong magnet-school programs in the Twin Cities since the late 1960s. It adopted a postsecondary options plan in 1985 and became the nation's first to adopt a phased-in statewide open enrollment policy in 1987. The state also operates a "second-chance" program for high school dropouts. About 13,000 of the state's 749,000 students participated in the open-enrollment plan in 1991–92. Few districts have gained or lost significant numbers of students, however, and choice's impact on the quality of instruction has been inconclusive.

## MISSISSIPPI

Gov. Kirk Fordice has proposed a pilot "choice" program. But state education officials say choice would prove difficult in a rural state where transportation costs run far ahead of available funding, severe local funding inequities exist, and the social climate and racial history "raise much suspicion about school choice."

## MISSOURI

Voters last November rejected by a 2–1 margin an education funding reform package that included statewide choice. For many years, districts with only elementary programs gave students the choice of attending any school in an approved district in the county of residence, or an adjacent county. Both Kansas City and St. Louis have operated interdistrict programs designed to achieve racial balance. Under the court-ordered plan in St. Louis, some thirteen thousand students attend schools of their choosing outside their districts.

## MONTANA

Choice is not deemed a meaningful statewide option for most of the 155,000 students in a sprawling rural state of 147,000 square miles. For years, the state has allowed students to attend other districts, however, and receiving districts may or may not charge tuition. A lack of state transportation subsidies makes choice unrealistic for most residents.

## NEBRASKA

In 1989, the legislature adopted a statewide interdistrict "choice" plan which currently involves 3,300 students. Transferring students have to wait 90 days before participating in interscholastic athletics. All but poor parents are required to pay for transportation to the receiving district. Unless they move, students can only change districts once prior to graduation.

106

## Nevada

Legislators may consider choice in the 1993 session. State education officials predict "a hard-fought battle," particularly if the plan includes private schools.

## New Hampshire

In October 1991 a policy statement from the state board of education supported school choice, but left action up to local districts. Portsmouth voters turned down a choice referendum by a margin of 5 to 1. A state-wide proposal allowing dissatisfied parents to send their child to "any state-approved school" may be sent to the state Supreme Court for an opinion on its constitutionality.

## New Jersey

A wide-ranging "choice" initiative promoted by former Gov. Thomas Kean was stalled by the 1990 budget shortfall. A pilot program was proposed in 1988 but received no funding. Pending legislation would provide a minimum level of state funding to follow students transferring to schools outside their districts. But it would include private schools, and participation by districts would be optional.

Montclair operates a nationally acclaimed magnet-school program, and Newark, Atlantic City, and Franklin Township also have extensive magnet-school choice programs.

## New Mexico

Since 1978, state law has allowed local districts to admit nonresident students, if space is available. State aid follows the student, but the receiving districts are only responsible for transporting students within their own borders. The state also has a postsecondary options program and numerous intradistrict "choice" plans.

## New York

Although there is no legislatively prescribed plan, the Board of Regents' "New Compact for Learning" embraced choice and committed the state to removing any administrative obstacles. The board last summer rejected nonpublic school choice. Locally, East Harlem's District 4 and several other Manhattan districts have extensive open enrollment programs. In September 1992, New York City's school chancellor, Joseph Fernandez, proposed allowing elementary and junior high school children to attend any school they wish in any of the city's 32 local districts beginning in the fall of 1993. Buffalo and Yonkers have long-standing magnet-school programs, and Rochester and Buffalo operate urban-suburban transfer programs allowing for interdistrict choice to achieve racial balance. The state provides transportation for participating students.

## North Carolina

Choice has not yet surfaced as a statewide issue.

## North Dakota

Early discussions are under way for a possible statewide plan similar to Minnesota's pioneering open enrollment system. There is great concern, however, that choice would increase pressures to consolidate or close the state's many small schools.

## Ohio

The state's current interdistrict law gives local districts the option of participating. So far, only 115 students have transferred. Beginning in July 1993, state law requires all districts to adopt intradistrict "choice" policies, as well as policies either prohibiting all student transfers from adjacent districts or allowing such transfers to occur tuition-free. A 1991 state report predicted that open enrollment is not likely to result in massive student movement.

## OKLAHOMA

The legislature has failed so far to pass an open enrollment plan. Among the problems cited by state officials is the lack of funding for transportation. Many districts have intradistrict programs, however.

## OREGON

State officials say that 5 percent of Oregon's roughly 500,000 students are in inter- and intradistrict "choice" programs that were enacted in 1991. In July 1992, the state board of education issued guidelines to help districts that want to establish programs. Extensive programs already exist in Eugene and Portland.

## PENNSYLVANIA

In December 1991, legislators rejected, by a 114–89 vote, a plan allowing students to attend any public, private, or parochial school they wished and providing $900 tuition vouchers.

## RHODE ISLAND

Choice has not assumed a significant role in this state. There is no law mandating statewide choice, but thirty-two hundred students take part in local school option plans in fourteen of the state's thirty-seven districts. More than twenty-four hundred of those students are in Providence.

## SOUTH CAROLINA

Choice remains entirely a local school district option. A few districts, notably Richland School District Two, are experimenting with their own plans.

## SOUTH DAKOTA

Choice hasn't surfaced as a major school reform issue in this sparsely populated state. However, the state has one of the nation's more liberal home schooling guidelines: in 1990–91, some 400 home schools served 727 students, and 39 church-sponsored schools served another 731.

## TENNESSEE

Choice has a seventy-year history in this state. State law allows any student to attend the school nearest home, even if that school lies outside the student's district. Transferring students are responsible for transportation costs. The state estimates that twenty-two thousand students attended schools outside their home districts in 1991.

## TEXAS

Legislators are studying a variety of options, including allowing state funding to follow students to non-public schools. Several districts, notably Garland and Houston, operate extensive magnet-school programs.

## UTAH

A statewide ''choice'' law enacted in 1991 cleared the way for inter- and intradistrict programs which now involve an estimated four- to five-thousand students. The state is considering providing funding for interdistrict transportation.

## VERMONT

For more than a hundred years, the state has allowed students from districts without a public high school to attend public or non-public schools, with taxpayers paying all or part of the cost. There are eighty such districts, most of them quite small. Some lawmakers now favor excluding high-cost prep schools from the program.

## VIRGINIA

The state is in the midst of a three-phase study of possible statewide "choice" programs. Virginia operates one of the nation's only statewide magnet-school programs, the "Virginia Governor's Schools," with sixty-two schools. Portsmouth operates a system of magnet high schools, and Roanoke has twenty-nine magnet-school programs.

## WASHINGTON

A "Learning by Choice" program adopted in 1990 required all districts to establish policies allowing students to transfer within districts and giving them wider freedom to transfer to any district in the state; established a phased-in "Running Start" program allowing eleventh- and twelfth-graders to enroll in community colleges and vocational institutes while attending high school; and created a seventh- and eighth-grade program allowing students to earn high school credits at schools of their choice.

As of October 1991, twenty-four thousand students were involved in intradistrict "choice" programs. Another 9,900 were in interdistrict plans, 575 were in "Running Start," and 5,839 were in seventh- and eighth-grade choice.

## WEST VIRGINIA

The state has no provision for school choice, but students can attend schools in an adjoining county where space is available and when both school boards agree to the transfer.

## WISCONSIN

The Milwaukee Parental Choice Program passed by state lawmakers in 1990 is the nation's only local school choice plan allowing public school children to attend private school at taxpayer expense. The controversial plan provides about $2,600 per student for up to a thousand poor students to attend qualified non-sectarian private schools. Some 632 students participated in the fall of 1992.

Gov. Tommy Thompson has thus far failed to get a number of other statewide plans through the legislature, including interdistrict choice and postsecondary options.

## WYOMING

Choice is not a burning issue in this state, particularly since the school population is low and the distances between schools are great. However, state officials say that district boundaries are often ignored.

# APPENDIX D

## *Technical Notes*

THE CARNEGIE FOUNDATION for the Advancement of Teaching sponsored three surveys as part of this study.

To gather information on school choice in each state, the Foundation administered a national survey of chief state school officers in March 1992. Questionnaires were mailed to all fifty states and the District of Columbia, and fifty-one responses were received, representing a completion rate of 100 percent. A follow-up survey was conducted in August to obtain updated information.

In July and August 1992, The Wirthlin Group of McLean, Virginia, administered a telephone survey to 1,013 parents with children attending public schools. Respondents were asked to provide information about the schools their children attend, the distance to other schools, and the modes of transportation used to reach the schools.

The Wirthlin Group also administered a telephone survey of public opinion in September 1992, asking 1,005 individuals to respond to a question concerning public school reform strategies.

As with all surveys, the results of these surveys are subject to sampling variations. The magnitude of these variations is measurable, and is affected by a number of factors, including the number of respondents and the distribution of responses to any given question. For example, where 50 percent of the respondents in a group of one thousand choose a certain answer to a question, the chances are 95 in 100 that if the entire population were asked the same question using the same survey procedures, the result would vary by no more than plus or minus 3 percentage points.

Additional information on the data presented in this report can be obtained from The Carnegie Foundation for the Advancement of Teaching, Data and Trends Analysis, 5 Ivy Lane, Princeton, New Jersey 08540.

# NOTES

CHAPTER 1    *Freedom to Choose*

1. Joe Nathan, ''Results and Future Prospects of State Efforts to Increase Choice Among Schools,'' *Phi Delta Kappan,* Vol. 68, No. 10, June 1987, p. 748.

2. Jeanne Allen and Angela Hulsey, *School Choice Programs: What's Happening in the States* (Washington, D.C.: The Heritage Foundation, 1992), p. 1.

3. ''American Education Week Debate: Resolved—Freedom to Choose Means Better Schools,'' transcript of proceedings before the U.S. Department of Education, Capital Hill Reporting (official reporters), 13 Nov. 1990, p. 16.

4. U.S. Department of Education, ''Secretary Lamar Alexander on Choice in Education,'' 19 June 1992; citing *The Washington Post,* 10 Feb. 1992.

5. Ruth Randall and Keith Geiger, *School Choice: Issues & Answers* (Bloomington, Ind.: National Educational Service, 1991), p. 9.

6. U.S. Department of Education, ibid., citing *Parade Magazine*, 25 Aug. 1991.

7. Joe Nathan, p. 750.

8. John E. Chubb and Terry M. Moe, *Politics, Markets, and America's Schools* (Washington, D.C.: Brookings Institution, 1990), p. 216.

9. Ibid., p. 198.

10. Office of Educational Research and Improvement (OERI), U.S. Department of Education, *Getting Started: How Choice Can Renew Your Pub-*

*lic Schools* (Washington, D.C.: U.S. Government Printing Office, Aug. 1992), p. 1.

11. Chubb and Moe, p. 217.

12. William Kolberg, ''Choice Can't Stand Alone,'' *WorkAmerica*, National Alliance of Business, Washington, D.C., Vol. 8, No. 4, April 1991, p. 3.

13. Albert Shanker, ''Bush's New Voucher Program: G.I. Bull,'' *The New Republic*, 27 July 1992, Vol. 207, No. 30, p. 23.

14. National PTA, position statement on parental choice, as requested by the U.S. Department of Education, 5 Sept. 1989.

15. Chubb and Moe, p. 217.

CHAPTER 2    *School Choice: Possibilities and Problems*

1. Stanley M. Elam, Lowell C. Rose, and Alec M. Gallup, ''The 23rd Annual Gallup Poll of the Public's Attitudes Toward the Public Schools,'' *Phi Delta Kappan*, Vol. 73, No. 1, Sept. 1991, pp. 47–48.

2. Howard Goldberg, ''Majority in AP Poll Backs Grants for Parental School Choice,'' the Associated Press, 6 September 1992.

3. Arizona Department of Education, ''Results of the Non-Resident Student Enrollment Survey,'' Research and Development, 13 Dec. 1989.

4. The Carnegie Foundation for the Advancement of Teaching, Survey of Chief State School Officers, 1992; see Appendix C.

5. Minnesota House of Representatives, ''Open Enrollment Study: Student and District Participation, 1989–90, Working Paper #1,'' Feb. 1990, Research Department, p. 2.

6. Michael C. Rubinstein, Rosalind Hamar, Nancy E. Adelman, ''Minnesota's Open Enrollment Option,'' Policy Studies Associates, Inc., Washington, D.C.; prepared for the U.S. Department of Education, contract LC89089001, 1992, pp. 30, 35–36.

7. Ibid., pp. 13–14.

8. Millicent Lawton, "Gallup Poll Finds Wide Support for Tuition Vouchers," *Education Week*, Vol. 12, No. 3, 23 Sept. 1992, pp. 1, 16.

9. Mary Driscoll, "Changing Minds and Changing Hearts: Choice, Achievement and School Community," paper delivered at a symposium on school choice sponsored by the Economic Policy Institute, Washington, D.C., 1 Oct. 1992, p. 15.

10. Lauren A. Sosniak and Corinna A. Ethington, "When Public School 'Choice' Is Not Academic: Findings from the National Education Longitudinal Study of 1988," *Educational Evaluation and Policy Analysis*, Vol. 14, No. 1, Spring 1992, pp. 35–52.

11. Ibid., p. 49.

12. Office of Educational Research and Improvement (OERI), U.S. Department of Education, *Getting Started: How Choice Can Renew Your Public Schools,* (Washington, D.C.: U.S. Government Printing Office, Aug. 1992), p. 29.

13. Ibid., p. 26.

14. Ibid., p. 25.

CHAPTER 3   *Districtwide Choice: Montclair, Cambridge, East Harlem*

1. Beatriz C. Clewell and Myra F. Joy, *Choice in Montclair, New Jersey* (Princeton, N.J.: Educational Testing Service, 1990), p. 9.

2. Barbara Strobert, "Factors Influencing Parental Choice in Selecting Magnet Schools in the Montclair, New Jersey, Public Schools," dissertation for Teachers College, Columbia University, 1990, pp. 46–47.

3. Ibid., p. 49.

4. Ibid., pp. 47–48.

5. Ibid., p. 77, table 5.

6. Ibid., p. 79.

7. Bell Associates, Inc., "A Study of Parent Attitudes Toward the Cambridge Public Schools," Cambridge, Mass., 13 September 1988.

8. Ibid., pp. 6–20.

9. Ibid., p. 22.

10. Lee Mitgang, "Cavazos' Choice Pitch Gets Tangled in East Harlem School Funding," The Associated Press, 17 October 1989.

11. John E. Chubb and Terry M. Moe, *Politics, Markets, and America's Schools* (Washington, D.C.: Brookings Institution, 1990), p. 212.

12. Alvarado's term as schools chancellor ended in financial scandal in 1984. He has since become superintendent of Manhattan's District 2, where he has moved aggressively to introduce school choice.

13. Interview with Carlos Medina, Fellow of The Manhattan Institute. Medina was Alvarado's successor as District 4's superintendent and served from 1982 to 1988.

14. Jeanne Allen and Angela Hulsey, *School Choice Programs: What's Happening in the States* (Washington, D.C.: The Heritage Foundation, 1992), p. 19.

15. Rankings are based on data drawn from the New York City Board of Education's "OREA Report: Spring 1992 Results, Reading and Mathematics Achievement." It should be noted that the falloff in East Harlem's scores after 1987 was typical citywide and is explainable in part by the renorming in 1988 of the Degrees of Reading Power test used to measure student reading ability in New York City. Central board officials blamed the citywide declines in 1992 on sharp budget cuts. Two critical points remain, however: District 4's average scores remain well below the citywide average, and its relative standing in reading ability among the city's thirty-two local districts has slipped since 1987.

16. Rankings are based on data drawn from the New York City Board of Education's "OREA Report: Spring 1992 Results, Reading and Mathematics Achievement."

17. District 4, "Reading Summary Statistics—Spring, Alternative Schools 1991," pp. 5–6, and "Summary Statistics—Spring 1991: Mathematics," pp. 6–8.

CHAPTER 4   *Statewide Choice: Winners and Losers*

1.  National Governors' Association, *Time for Results: The Governors' 1991 Report on Education*, Washington, D.C., August 1986, p. 12.

2.  The Carnegie Foundation for the Advancement of Teaching, Survey of Chief State School Officers, 1992; see Appendix C.

3.  Superintendent of Public Instruction, State of Washington, ''Choice Enrollment Survey,'' October 1991, p. 2.

4.  Even if one stretched the meaning of ''choice'' to include interdistrict options such as postsecondary enrollment, dropout programs, area learning centers, and alternative programs, only about 4 percent of Minnesota's students are involved in such transfers.

5.  David Bechtel, ''Open Enrollment: Preliminary Report for the 1989–90 and 1990–91 School Years,'' Iowa State Department of Education, table 5, p. 15.

6.  Arizona Department of Education, ''Results of the Non-Resident Student Enrollment Survey,'' Research and Development, 13 Dec. 1989.

7.  Michael C. Rubinstein, Rosalind Hamar, Nancy E. Adelman, ''Minnesota's Open Enrollment Option,'' Policy Studies Associates, Inc., Washington, D.C.; prepared for the U.S. Department of Education, contract LC89089001, 1992, pp. 30, 35–36.

8.  Mary Jane Smetanka, ''Schools Changing Under Student Choice Program,'' *Star Tribune* (Minneapolis), 16 Dec. 1991, p. 1; according to this article, ''educators say the number of high schools offering advanced-placement courses has increased several times over.''

9.  The College Board, *School Report of 1992 Advanced Placement Examinations (by State)*, New York.

10. Minnesota House of Representatives, ''Open Enrollment Study: Survey of School District Superintendents, 1989–90, Working Paper #2,'' Research Department, Jan. 1991, p. 5.

11. Michael C. Rubinstein, Rosalind Hamar, Nancy E. Adelman, ''Minnesota's Open Enrollment Option,'' Policy Studies, Inc., Washington,

D.C.; prepared for the U.S. Department of Education, contract LC89089001, 1992, p. 50.

12. Ibid., pp. 47–48.

13. Lewis W. Finch, "The Claims for School Choice and Snake Oil Have a Lot in Common," *The American School Board Journal*, July 1989, p. 31.

14. Susan Andersen, "School Choice Will Equalize," letters to the editor, *The Berkshire Eagle*, 8 April 1982.

15. Charles L. Glenn, "Creating an Irresponsible School Choice Program," a paper prepared for the 1992 Politics of Education Association Yearbook, p. 31.

16. Data gathered by State Sen. Arthur E. Chase, R-Worcester.

17. Ibid.

18. Richard Fossey, *School Transportation and School Choice in Massachusetts: A Report to the Legislature submitted by the Commissioner of Education* (Cambridge: Harvard University Graduate School of Education, 1992), pp. 23–24.

19. Mary Ann Raywid, "Choice Orientations, Discussions and Prospects," *Educational Policy*, Vol. 6, No. 2, June 1992, p. 117.

20. "States' School-Spending Disparities," *Education Week*, 17 June 1992, p. 28; source listed as state education departments, 1990–91 and 1989–90 figures.

21. Charles L. Glenn, pp. 35–36.

CHAPTER 5 *Private-School Choice: Milwaukee*

1. Clifford Krauss, "Senate Rejects Bush Plan to Aid the Poor Who Use Private Schools," *The New York Times*, 24 Jan. 1992, p. 15.

2. Stanley M. Elam, Lowell C. Rose, and Alec M. Gallup, "The 23rd Annual Gallup Poll of the Public's Attitudes Toward the Public

Schools,'' *Phi Delta Kappan*, Vol. 73, No. 1, Sept. 1991, p. 47. The question was worded: ''In some nations, the government allots a certain amount of money for each child's education. The parents can then send the child to any public, parochial, or private school they choose. This is called the 'voucher system.' Would you like to see such an idea adopted in this country?''

3.  Millicent Lawton, ''Gallup Poll Finds Wide Support for Tuition Vouchers,'' *Education Week*, Vol. 12, No. 3, 23 Sept. 1992, pp. 1, 16.

4.  ''Los Angeles, Chicago Lawsuits Demand Private School Choice,'' *Education Daily*, Vol. 25, No. 111, 10 June 1992, p. 1.

5.  U.S. Department of Education, ''Secretary Lamar Alexander on Choice in Education,'' 19 June 1992; citing press release of 10 June 1992.

6.  John F. Witte, *First Year Report: Milwaukee Parental Choice Program*, Department of Political Science and The Robert M. La Follette Institute of Public Affairs, University of Wisconsin, Madison, Nov. 1991, p. 24.

7.  John F. Witte, ''The Milwaukee Private-School Parental Choice Program,'' Department of Political Science, University of Wisconsin, Madison; paper given at the Economic Policy Institute Conference, Washington, D.C., 1 October 1992, table 3.

8.  Ibid., pp. 18–19.

9.  Interview with John F. Witte, 14 Oct. 1992.

10.  Data reported by the district's department of financial services.

11.  Excerpt from opinion by Wisconsin State Supreme Court Justice Shirley S. Abrahamson, Davis et al. v. Grover, 90–1807 (3 March 1992), p. 4.

CHAPTER 6  *In Search of Common Ground*

1.  Nathan Glazer, ''No Excuse for Failure: Urban Schools in Transition,'' *The City Journal* (CUNY), Vol. 2, No. 4, August 1992, p. 27.

2.  Robert W. Carr, ''Markets Can't Fix Schools' Problems,'' *The Wall Street Journal*, 2 May 1991, p. 17.

3.   "Students Still Coming to School Unready to Learn, Teachers Say," *Education Daily,* Vol. 25, No. 178, 15 Sept. 1992; citing The Metropolitan Life Survey of the American Teacher 1992.

CHAPTER 7   *School Choice in Perspective*

1.   In Merle Curti, *The Social Ideas of American Educators* (Lanham, MD: Littlefield, Adams and Co., 1959), p. 198.

2.   David Rockefeller, Jr., "America 2000 and Philanthropy's Education Agenda," *Teachers College Record,* Vol. 93, No. 3, Spring 1992, p. 374.

3.   In Curti, p. 47

4.   Thomas Jefferson, *The Jefferson Writings,* ed. Merrill Peterson (New York: Library of America, 1984), p. 460; and letter to P. S. du Pont de Nemours, 24 April 1816, *The Writings of Thomas Jefferson,* ed. Paul L. Ford, Vol. 10, p. 25 (1899).

5.   In Christopher Lasch, *The Culture of Narcissism: American Life in an Age of Diminishing Expectations* (New York: Warner Books, 1979), pp. 231–32; citing Michael Chevalier, *Society, Manners, and Politics in the United States: Letters on North America* (New York: Doubleday, 1961 [1838]), ch. 34.

6.   In Curti, p. 132.

7.   Lawrence A. Cremin, *American Education: The Metropolitan Experience, 1876–1980* (New York: Harper & Row, 1988), p. 649; emphasis ours.

8.   Robert N. Bellah et al., *Habits of the Heart: Individualism and Commitment in American Life* (Berkeley: University of California Press, 1985), p. 37; citing Alexis de Tocqueville, *Democracy in America,* trans. George Lawrence, ed. J. P. Mayer (New York: Doubleday, Anchor Books, 1969), p. 287.

9.   Ibid., p. viii.

10.   Ibid., p. 21.

# INDEX

# INDEX